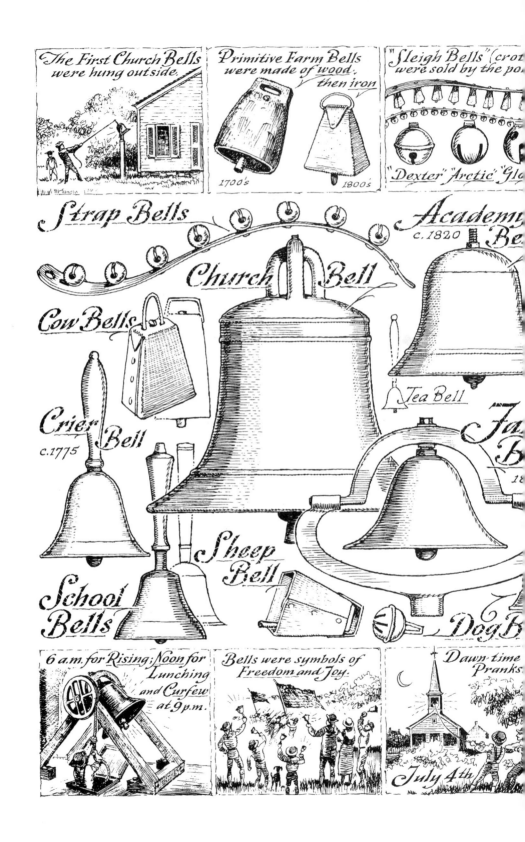

The First Church Bells were hung outside.

Primitive Farm Bells were made of wood, then iron
1700's 1800's

"Sleigh Bells" (crot were sold by the po
"Dexter" "Arctic" "Glo

Strap Bells

Academy
Be
c.1820

Cow Bells

Church Bell

Crier Bell
c.1775

Tea Bell

Ja
B
18

School Bells

Sheep Bell

Dog B

6 a.m. for Rising; Noon for Lunching and Curfew at 9 p.m.

Bells were symbols of Freedom and Joy.

Dawn-time Pranks

July 4th

# A CELEBRATION of BELLS

*Eric Sloane* and *Eric Hatch*

DOVER PUBLICATIONS, INC.
Mineola, New York

*Bibliographical Note*

*A Celebration of Bells,* first published in 2008, is an unabridged republication, in one volume, of *The Little Book of Bells* by Eric Hatch and Eric Sloane, originally published by Duell, Sloan and Pearce, New York, in 1964; and *The Sound of Bells* by Eric Sloane, originally published by Doubleday & Company, Inc., Garden City, New York, in 1966.

*Library of Congress Cataloging-in-Publication Data*

Sloane, Eric.
    A celebration of bells / Eric Sloane and Eric Hatch.
        p. cm.
    An unabridged republication, is one volume, of The little book of bells by Eric Hatch and Eric Sloane, originally published by Duell, Sloan, and Pearce, New York, N.Y., in 1964; and The sound of bells, originally published by Doubleday, Garden City, N.Y., in 1966.
    ISBN-13: 978-0-486-46826-6
    ISBN-10: 0-486-46826-7
    1. Bells—History. I. Hatch, Eric, 1901–1973. II. Hatch, Eric, 1907–1973. Little book of bells. III. Sloane, Eric. Sound of bells. IV. Title.

CC205.S58 2008
786.8'84819—dc22

2008048694

Manufactured in the United States of America
Dover Publications, Inc., 31 East 2nd Street, Mineola, N.Y. 11501

# The Little Book of Bells

Eric Hatch

with sketches
by Eric Sloane

*In appreciation of the wise counsel and friendship*
*Which made it possible*
*This book is dedicated to*

## DR. ALFRED F. RIZZOLO

# Contents

# Foreword

In the early afternoon of July 4 last year, I drove to Torrington, Connecticut. The short trip was made alone; I would have had it no other way. The downtown section of the city was deserted for the holiday except for an occasional car passing slowly along Main Street. I parked at an intersection in front of a department store whose window was devoted to a display of American flags, colonial documents, and bells.

I turned on the radio on the seat beside me, tuning in to a network station and toning the sound down to a whisper. Then I sat quietly and waited. The minutes passed. At 2 P.M., daylight-saving time, the almost complete silence of the city was broken. Church bells, first one and then another, sent their shimmering, silvery sounds echoing from the belfries. A moment before the radio had been broadcasting a ball game from Chicago, but this had been interrupted. In its place came the sound of bells from the state Capitol. I switched from station to station. From each came the peal of bells.

Feeling a little self-conscious and even a little foolish

though I was alone, I picked up the replica of the Williamsburgh Town Crier's Bell I had brought with me. I rang it. And I knew that in every state of the Union, in every major city, and in thousands of towns and villages across the land and around the world the bells of America were ringing a massive salute to the memory of the men who had given us freedom. I wanted to be a part of it. I rang my little bell and shamelessly wept with emotion.

This moment was the culmination of many months of effort. It all began when Eric Sloane and I joined in what was to become a project of patriotism. All our energies were to be devoted to a precisely timed national ringing of the bells. With the help of governors, state legislatures, individuals, and organizations of every kind, we had sown the wind. And the breezes of a summer day were to carry our message around the world.

When we set out on this mission, I realized that in the weeks and months ahead I should find myself in daily contact with bell-ringers and bell owners, and so I determined to learn something about their subject. I don't know what happened then. Perhaps some ancient temple bell whose vast vibrations still throb faintly on quiet winter nights cast a spell over me. I became enchanted with bells. And now I wish to share my small knowledge in the hope that others will also be touched by a little of the same magic.

E. H.

# 1.
## How the Bells Began

Flat dish . . Skirted dish . . Dish bell . . BELL!

The bell was probably discovered by accident when primitive man began working with metals. The first resonance may have been caused by the striking of a metal dish. The edges of that dish were then gradually bent down to form skirts. And a crude version of the shape now so familiar was first fashioned.

True bell-making, however, did not come until man learned to make bronze by mixing copper and tin. An early bell of the bronze period was the quadrangular bell. Made from two bent plates of sheet iron and fastened together with iron rivets, this structure was then coated with bronze.

A bell of this type that remains intact today is the *Clog-an-eadhacta Phatraic* or "The Bell of the Will of St. Patrick." This little bell, 6 inches high, 4¾ inches wide at the shoulder, and 5 inches across at the base, is rung by hand. As its sound must be frightful, this may have been St. Patrick's secret weapon. No snake, if he were at all like the oriental snakes and addicted to sweet flute music, would have remained in Ireland and listened to the racket St. Patrick must have made when he rang his *Clog-an-eadhacta*. According to the *Annals of Ulster*, this bell was removed from St. Patrick's tomb by

the Ll Llanrwst Bell

the St. Patrick's Bell

c. 450 A.D

St. Colomoille in A.D. 552 and is now preserved with its shrine in the National Museum of Ireland.

With the establishment of the Bronze Age, bells were taken seriously. (The actual business of making them has been traced back to 2697 B.C.) They were cast in molds, and though each bell had a resonance, once in a while, almost as if by accident, one emerged with a true tone of some beauty. But the arrival at anything approximating present bells was a long way off.

Much more rapid was the development of a totally different type of bell, whose contours and tone quality have remained the same throughout the ages. Known for millenniums as the Crotal, this bell is a little sphere with small holes in its sides and a tiny ball, originally of stone, now of metal, inside it. The sleigh bell is an example of this type; and today one may find these Crotal bells on Christmas trees, on children's rattles, or on the ankles of Pueblo Indian dancers.

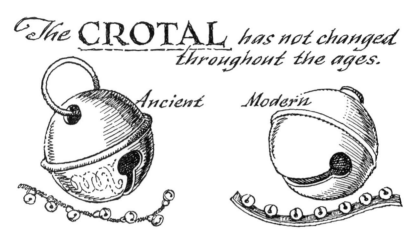

The CROTAL has not changed throughout the ages.

Ancient          Modern

Beyond any doubt these Crotals are the same little golden bells referred to in Exodus XXVIII:33–34 as those commanded to be made for the adornment of Ephod of Aaron: "Upon the hem pomegranates of blue, and of purple, and of scarlet: . . . and bells of gold between them round about; a golden bell and a pomegranate, a golden bell and a pomegranate." The Crotal is a true bell form and is the most ancient of all forms. The marked resemblance between the ancient and modern Crotal is extraordinary. I cannot think of any other object that was created thousands of years ago in a form so perfect that no one since has been able to find a way of improving it.

The first bells to be foundry-cast in the western world did not appear until the late sixth or early seventh century. In the Orient the art of bell-making was much further advanced. The same emperor who built the Great Wall of China in 220 B.C. is mentioned by historians as having cast huge bells. And at one time in the dim mists of ancient history, the Great Bell of Pekin was cast. This bell may be as old as four thousand years. Huge for its day, large for any day, it was 14½ feet high and 13 feet around. It was a straight-sided bell up to the curve at the top.

In Europe the art of bell-making came much later. It reached its peak at the time in the twelfth or thirteenth century when bells assumed their present shape. At that time the addition of the "sound bow," that thick part just above the bottom edge of the lip where the clapper strikes, added immeasurably to the bell's tunability and resonance. The shape of these bells, like that of the Crotal, has scarcely been improved to this day.

There was, however, one more major development, although not in the bell itself. This came in the nineteenth century with the invention of a tuning machine, really no more than a vertical lathe. The process of bell-tuning then became scientific.

I never realized until I began visiting research libraries that bells were tuned. I thought they just rang. I knew that molds of some sort were made in the shape of a bell; metal was poured into them; and then, having had time to cool, the outside of these molds was removed; and there was the bell.

I thought some bells turned out treble and some bass, some dissonant and some true. I couldn't have been more mistaken. Even in the old days a bell-founder setting out to cast a "ring" or set of bells would try to shape them so that they would all have different notes, yet all emerge from the mold exactly in tune with each other, in harmony. Maybe once in a lifetime he'd be successful. When he was, it became a cause for wild celebration, and the peal he had cast was known as

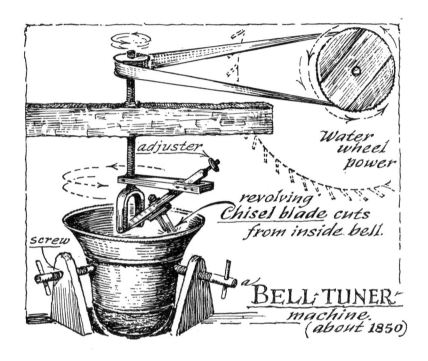

*adjuster*

*screw*

*Water wheel power*

*revolving Chisel blade cuts from inside bell.*

a *BELL TUNER machine.*
*(about 1850)*

a "virgin ring." Such a bell-founder would not think highly of any tuned bell if the tuning were done by hacking away at the metal of the bell near the lip edge with a hammer and chisel. This process was laborious, slow, and noisy almost beyond endurance. However, one Englishman named Laurence Huddlestone, who was a bell-tuner by trade, spent his life going about with his hammer and chisel from church to church; and when he found bells whose sound was wrong, without asking anyone he simply went to work and tuned them.

At first glance this science of tuning bells might appear to

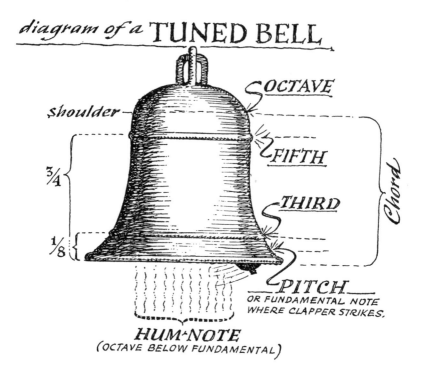

diagram of a TUNED BELL

shoulder

OCTAVE

¾

FIFTH

THIRD

Chord

⅛

PITCH
OR FUNDAMENTAL NOTE
WHERE CLAPPER STRIKES.

HUM-NOTE
(OCTAVE BELOW FUNDAMENTAL)

be of interest only to tintinnabulologists, campanologists, carillonneurs, change ringers, and sextons. This is far from true, particularly when you consider a carillon such as the one at Riverside Church in New York City. This carillon is composed of seventy-two separate bells and is probably the most public musical instrument in the world. Consider, too, that a tuned bell doesn't sound just one note. It sounds a chord of five notes. When you take into account the number of people who live within hearing distance of 490 Riverside Drive, thousands of people who don't even know they are interested in bell-tuning, you can see why any self-respecting carillonneur would feel just a little embarrassed if his bells were not in tune. After all, with five notes to a bell, the carillon totals 360 separate notes; and to make things tougher, the bourdon, or tenor bell, in the Riverside carillon has thirteen recognizable tones–recognizable to a carillonneur, that is.

To understand how one bell produces all these different notes, we must consider harmonics. An harmonic is described in Webster's dictionary as: "an overtone, esp. one produced by a vibration or frequency which is an integral multiple of the vibration rate producing the fundamental."

The Rev. George S. Tyack, of England wrote in 1898:

> A bell in perfect tune sounds a perfect chord. There is the note struck out directly by the clapper from the sound bow; this booms out most prominently and if the pitch of the bell be spoken of, it is this tone to which reference is made. But as the vibrations of the stroke set the whole mass of metal throbbing, the following notes are also sounded; at one eighth of the height of the bell from the brim, a third above the fundamental note is given; at three quarters of the height, a fifth; and at the shoulder the chord is completed by the octave. Besides these there is also developed from them the "hum note," as it is called, consisting of the note an octave below the fundamental.

This is the Simpson Principle of bell-tuning. The old system was to tune to the natural harmonics of the strike note with the hum note a seventh below. Here is the sheet music for tuning a bell:

This seems thoroughly convincing, yet to my surprise it is a very controversial subject. Some carillonneurs angrily cry out, "Not so!" Others say, "You have to watch old Tyack—very frivolous chap!" But I'm going to stick to the Tyack version for the origin of noises, as the dissenters seem reluctant to make a flat statement as to just how, in their opinion, the chord is formed.

# 2.

## the BIGGEST BELL in the world.

The biggest bell ever made never uttered a sound. However, if this book finds its way behind the iron curtain, I wouldn't be surprised if a few billion rubles weren't spent in a belated attempt to make it ring. But this would present a problem, not only because eleven tons of the bell are missing, but also because, even without that, it weighs roughly 423,000 pounds.

This behemoth of bells was cast by a founder named Michael Motorine in 1734, during the reign of Empress Anne of Russia. It was 19 feet high, 22 ½ feet in diameter and just under 2 feet thick. Its clapper, or tongue, was 14 feet long and 6 feet in circumference at its extreme width. As would seem necessary for ringing such a monster, instead of the bell itself being swung, the clapper was supposed to be swung. Noblemen and others who were enthusiastic about making the biggest bell in the world eagerly contributed seventy thousand pounds of gold and silver to the melting pot. Unfortunately, however, bronze is best for bells; and these precious metals served only to deaden any potential tone.

In 1737, this impressive mass of metal was somehow actually lifted into the air and supended from a frame built of tremendous wooden beams at one end of the Kremlin. But the god that governs bells must have decided it was never to ring. A fire broke out in the Kremlin, ate its way to the belfry, and before it could be brought under control chewed away the supporting timbers. The bell, which was called the great Tsar Kolokol and nicknamed Ivan Kiliki or Big John, fell so mightily that it dug 30 feet into the ground. And there it lay for exactly a hundred years, a monument to its own unheard voice. Then, by means of block and tackle and the united efforts of six hundred soldiers, Tsar Kolokol was hoisted out of the ground and slid onto a pedestal. As a bell it was a failure; but it does make a very nice chapel, for which purpose it is still used.

The Russians claim this was the biggest bell in the world; it did not ring, however, and so it does not really count. They *may*, however, have broken the record with Tsar Kolokol's predecessor. First cast in 1654, this bell was later melted down, recast with additional metal, and became Tsar Kolokol. It weighed 260,000 pounds and *did* ring, with fifty men hauling its giant clapper, twenty-five to a side. But there is still another giant bell, hanging in a pagoda at Mingoon, in Burma. Closer in shape to a bell of the West than most Eastern bells, its weight has been estimated at ninety tons and upward. A certain Dr. Chill writing in *Travel Magazine* in October, 1896, said of this bell, "[it] . . . is the largest in the world (not excepting the well-known Russian bell in

*One way to ring a bell .. (Russian way)*

Moscow), and can easily hold within it a picnic party of fifty people." Well, that's one way of measuring bells.

Although Russia probably has more big bells than any other country, China also has a good many. Aside from the difference in shape, you can always tell an Eastern bell from a Western one by the fact that the Eastern one doesn't have

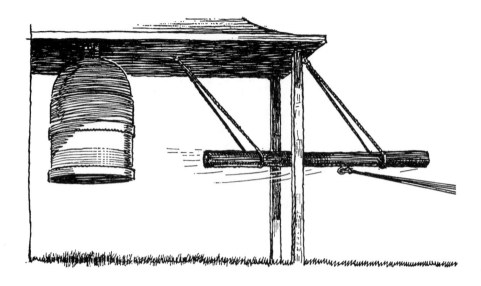

a clapper. Instead, mounted in the air beside it and suspended by ropes or chains in a horizontal position, is the trunk of a good-sized tree. To sound the bell, temple priests haul the trunk back as far as they can, then let her go. As the beam rebounds, they grab it. These big temple bells are called "the awakeners of Buddha," and their voices are deep, rich, mellow, and prolonged. The priests and the deeply religious believe implicitly that the sound of these chords and harmonics trembling on the air form the syllables, "*Na-ō-mi-to-fah*"—the soul of Asia calling out to the believers, "O Buddha, hail!"

Let us glance at some of the things Christians have believed about their bells. The following inscription appears on a medieval English bell:

FULGORA GRANGO, DISSIPITO VENTOS

or, in translation from the Latin:

## Another way of ringing a bell . . .

## (Oriental fashion)

"The lightning I shatter, the hurricane scatter."

And another, on a medieval bell at Otterham, Cornwall:

VOCE MEA VIVA DEPELLA CUNCTA NOCIVA

"With my living voice I drive away harmful things."

To show that this sort of inscription really was popular with the parishioners, here is a quotation from the *Golden Legend of Wynken de Worde*, an ancient printer:

> It is said, the evil spirytes, that ben in the regyon of thayre, doubte moche when they here the bells rongen: and this is the same why the bells rongen when it thondreth and when grete tempeste and outrages of wether happen, to the end that feinds and wycked spirytes should be abashed and flee, and cease the movynge of tempest.

Around 1562 the clergy were split on this matter of church bells abashing evil "spirytes" and causing them to quit blowing up a storm. The Most Reverend Pilkington, bishop of Durham, said ringing sacred bells for the above purpose was unlawful. As he put it:

> You know, when there was a storm or fearful weather, then we rang the holy bells; they were they that must make all things well; they must drive away the devil! But I tell you, if the holy bells would serve against the devil, or that he might be put away through their sound, no doubt we would soon banish him out of all England; for I think if all the bells of England should be rung together at a certain hour, there would be almost no place but some bells might be heard there, and so the devil should have no abiding place in England.

But the bishop of Malta did not agree and, as recently as 1852, in the midst of a howling gale ordered his church bells rung to drive the storm away. Also in the past century, the bishop of Chalons christened a peal of church bells and in the sermon that was part of the christening ritual said:

> The bells, placed like sentinels in the towers, watch over us, and turn away from us temptations of the enemy of our salvation, as well as storms and tempests.
>
> They speak and pray for us in our troubles, they inform Heaven of the necessity of earth.

The age of superstition in religion is partially past; and for the moment, at least, the imagined power of church bells over demons is forgotten. Church bells, however, still retain a very definite power over the minds and emotions of people, for their sounding has been a part of the ritual of most religions for fifteen hundred years. They have called man to worship, they have pealed at his marriage, and they have

# The PARTS of a BELL

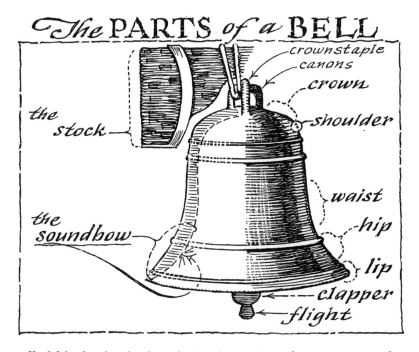

the stock

the soundbow

crownstaple
canons
crown
shoulder
waist
hip
lip
clapper
flight

tolled his death, ringing thrice three times for the death of a man, thrice two for the death of a woman, and then in slow measured strokes the number of years of life on earth.* They have rung man's alarms for fire, flood, and hurricane; and they have signaled peace at the end of his wars. When they ring they cannot help but cause some emotional reaction. For even in the simple striking of the hour by a familiar town clock, the chord of the bell strikes a chord in the mind of its hearer.

* The possible origin of this is found quoted in an English publication called *Manners and Customs*. "The fourme of the Trinity was founden in manne, that was Adam our forefadir, of earth, oon personne, and Eve of Adam the secunde persone, and of them both was the third persone: at the death of a manne three bellis shulde be ronge, as his knyll, in worscheppe of the Trinetee, and for the womanne, who was the secunde persone of the Trinetee two bellis should be rungen."

# 3

## The Bell of Port Royal

Today Jamaica is civilized and sophisticated. In the wintertime, Americans who want to switch from bourbon to rum or from sun lamps to sunshine, visit Kingston, Montego Bay, or several other Jamaican resorts. The island is now so cultivated that it is hard to remember that it was once one of the wildest spots in the world.

Kingston has a lovely, almost landlocked harbor. Yet Sir Henry Morgan, once admiral and governor of Jamaica, never heard of Kingston Harbor. It was Port Royal Harbor in the 1860's; and the town of Port Royal, on the tip of the curved point of land forming the sheltered harbor, was buccaneer capital of the Caribbean. It was bursting with wild men, loose women, captured Spanish silver and gold, and captive slaves, white as well as black. It was a prime town of sin; of pleasure for some, of deep anguish for others. These aspects of Port Royal have captured writers' imaginations and appear in their historical novels. That there was a church in Port Royal seems to have been entirely forgotten.

The church was a lovely one, with a bell tower made of well-fitted stones. It was a comfortable church to enter because there was always plenty of room for the congregation. The church bell had been cast in Spain; the parish priest who rang it maintained all the old traditions of the monastery where he had trained, religiously pulling away at the rope and ringing the hours. It gave him something to do and kept him from being lonely.

From time to time he used to go into the confessional and confess to himself of his angry thoughts and issue penances to himself. It was the only use the confessional got, for which in some ways he was thankful. His firm conviction was that if the whole population of Port Royal ever began confessing their sins, he would in short order get the notion he was dead and the Lord had committed him to hell. He prayed a great deal, mostly for strength, and often for the Lord to take violent vengeance on the sinners. After these prayers he would rush to the confessional. Praying for violence in a place that was already glutted with violence didn't seem Christian.

It was a long time before his prayers were answered, but they were. For on a very still and starshot night in the year sixteen hundred and ninety two, the bell in the stone tower of the Port Royal church began to ring. The sound was just a vibration at first, a soft tapping of the clapper against the bell as though someone were anxious to ring yet afraid of waking the town. Then the sound grew to a loud, measured

17

stroke that awakened the priest in his nearby house. He hurried to the church. But the church and the bell tower were empty, though the bell itself was now ringing with a wild, unbridled clanging; the rope was writhing and snapping like a dancing snake.

Pausing only to dip his fingers in the holy water of the font, the priest crossed himself and ran on, stumbling through the darkness and out of the town toward the mainland. Twenty years after the buccaneers had quieted down and four years after their prince, Sir Henry Morgan, had himself died there in Jamaica, the great vengeance had come. The few who had regularly heeded the voice of the bell did so now and followed the priest through the darkness.

The next morning the streets of Port Royal were cleansed of sin, washed clean by the warm, green waves of the Caribbean. And they would stay cleansed, for the ruins of the whole town were tumbled about on the ocean floor. The bell tower of the church still stood, however, its bell once again quiet. But tropical fish now moved in and out of the belfry, and occasional swells swayed the giant bell clapper ever so slightly.

The bell was quiet, but not quite silenced. Once again, two centuries later, it spoke its warning. This time it was only faintly heard or perhaps just imagined by the people of Kingston, a thriving town across the lovely harbor. But to the native fishermen, descendants of slaves brought to Port Royal so long ago, who were making their way to sea in their fragile canoes for the night's work, the warning of the bell beneath the sea was loud and real. In the manner of all primitive peoples, the story of the "earthquake bell" had been handed down from generation to generation. They *knew*, and they put back to port. In a matter of hours, earthquake and tidal wave had once again all but destroyed Kingston.

The next morning... ...the bell was silent.

That was in 1909. I believe the story because I have seen the bell tower looming mistily through the clear water, some twenty feet below the surface. I was rowed out to it by a native one morning in 1922. He knew about the bell ringing for the earthquake; he had heard it himself. For he was one of the fishermen who had been putting to sea that night. As he told me the story he dipped his fingers in the sea and crossed himself.

# 4
## Change Ringing.

Change ringers and carillonneurs are the aristocrats of the bell world. Both groups are so ancient that their history is almost lost in antiquity. Of the two, the carillonneurs who play tunes, hymns, and fugues are the more musical. The change ringers, however, are the more colorful. And to explain change ringing I must introduce a few basic facts.

The church bell is usually hung in a frame on an axle. The bell is rung by pulling on a rope that goes around a wheel fastened securely to the axle. This wheel has a groove the bell rope fits into, and at one point the rope passes

through to the inside of the wheel and is made fast to one of the spokes.

A *ring of bells*, often in change ringing called a *peal*, is a group of bells hung in the manner of an ordinary church bell except that they all rest upside down—they look like a nest of huge baby birds with their mouths open. A wooden device called a "stay," attached to the stock and resting against a "slider bar," keeps the bells from swinging over and maintains their balance in this upright position. The ringer pulls just hard enough so the bell will lose balance and swing down, strike, then rise up on the other side of its axle and remain there. The stay thus comes gently to rest against the opposite side of the slider. A very neat and acrobatic trick.

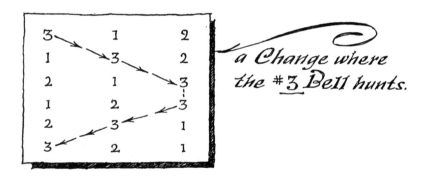

*a Change where the #3 Bell hunts.*

Change ringing is a trick of mathematics. If, for instance, you have a ring of three bells and you ring number one, then two, then three. you would not have rung a "change." But if you ring number two, then one, then three, you would have rung one change.

With a ring of three bells there are six possible changes.

You start ringing them in order, number one, number two, number three. This is called a "round."

In this example the number one bell is described as "hunting." * Switching places it goes from one end of the line to the other and then hunts its way back to where it began. This change, according to the language of the change ringers, is "true." You could of course do this in reverse and find the number three bell hunting. This pattern can also be repeated with the number two bell hunting, and at first glance it would appear that the mathematics quoted are incorrect and there are not six but eighteen possible changes from a set of three bells; but this is wrong. Change ringers for centuries have had their own laws and the second two sets are variations, not changes. In a contest the judge would throw these out as "false" since they contain repetitions, or "false course-ends."

Being able to ring three different bells six different ways does not seem like much of an accomplishment. But three bells are seldom used except for teaching the basic principles of change ringing. The first ring on record is the peal of *five* bells that Pope Calixt III sent to Kings College, Cambridge, in 1456 on which 120 changes were possible. (On a ring of seven bells, which is pretty standard, there are actually 5,040 potential changes. This is known as a triple.) At Kent School,

---

* The lingua obscura of change ringing is very difficult. The Reverend A. Gatty, M.A., as long ago as 1848 gave up trying to explain change-ringing terminology. Writing in *The Bell*, he said: " 'Great are the mysteries of bell ringing!' says Dr. Southey. 'The very terms are enough to frighten an amateur from any sort of explanation—*hunting, dodging, snapping*, and *place making; plain bobs, bob-triples, bob-majors*, and even up to *grandsire-bob-caters*. Heigho! Who can hope to translate all this gibberish to the uninitiated?' "

Connecticut, six bells out of a peal of ten are used; all six ring, each striking separately and distinctly, within only two seconds. The school's most impressive performance to date occurred during Easter, 1961, when it rang a "quarter peal"

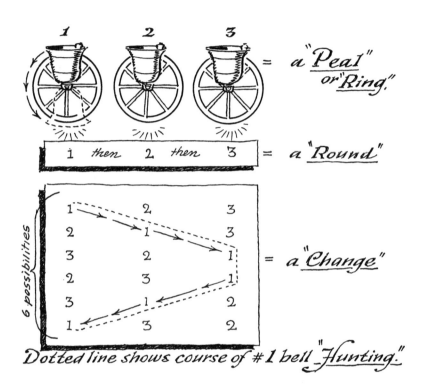

Dotted line shows course of #1 bell "Hunting."

totaling 1,260 changes. This took forty-five minutes of steady ringing, for there are no pauses between changes. To appreciate fully the physical and mental effort that can be put into change ringing, take the all-time record. On Saturday, July 21, 1923, at the Church of St. Chad in Cheshire, England, the Chester Diocesan Guild, consisting of eight ringers, rang a peal of Kent Treble Bob Major, which totaled an appalling 17,280 changes. This took them exactly ten hours and is the official record. What is remarkable is not only that eight men could ring these huge bells steadily for ten hours but also that they could ring that number of changes

| number of BELLS | Name of PEAL | Number of CHANGES |
|---|---|---|
| 4. | "Singles" | 24 |
| 5. | "Doubles" | 120 |
| 6. | "Minor" | 720 |
| 7. | "Triples" | 5,040 |
| 8. | "Major" | 40,320 |
| 9. | "Caters" | 362,880 |
| 10. | "Royal" | 3,628,800 |
| 11. | "Cinques" | 39,916,800 |
| 12. | "Maximus" | 479,001,600! |

surrounded by judges and timekeepers and not once ring a single bell at the wrong time or in the wrong order. There was one other ring of 18,240 changes completed by another group in eleven hours and thirteen minutes; but it didn't count, for somebody slipped and the composition was judged to be mathematically incorrect according to the rules of this ancient and weird ritual, because of false course-ends! On a maximus, or set of twelve bells, it would be mathematically possible to produce 479,001,600 changes. But this would take 137 years, and nobody's attention span is that long. But you are now able to see how change ringing can become a strange and fanatic pursuit.

At Kent School there is a change-ringing belfry patterned on the ancient belfries of England. It is a square room with bare walls and casement windows looking out over lovely, wooded hills. As one enters, by a flight of stone steps leading up from the chapel, he feels the dry coldness of an ancient castle tower. The ceiling is thirty feet high, and the room is quiet when the bells are not ringing.

The ropes hang in a somewhat circular pattern, with velvet handgrips nearly four feet long starting about five feet above the floor. The end of the rope is caught up in a loop rather suggestive of a hangman's noose. On my first visit I had no sooner gone into the ringing room than I was tempted by the handgrips. I walked to the nearest one and took hold. I just wanted to feel it, not pull it, but Mr. William Howard, my host, thought otherwise. I happened to glance at him as I reached up, and the horrified expression on his face made me freeze.

"*No!*" he cried in alarm. Then he explained that the bell at the other end of that rope weighed over a ton and was very delicately balanced. If I had given the rope a hard pull, the stay holding the bell in balance would have broken. The bell would have continued to ring; the wheel the rope was attached to would have spun around and gone right on spinning and, if I had not let go quickly, I should have been hoisted to the top of the belfry.

Considering this, I stepped well away from the rope.

Then I asked, "Mr. Howard, has this actually ever happened with the boys?"

He nodded. "Oh sure, but they're always warned about it when they start learning to ring. In spite of that, they still freeze to the grip occasionally and up they go."

"How high?"

"The thing at the other end of this rope weighs over a ton."

"Well," he said, "I've never seen one go up more than about eight feet. When the bells are hanging in the down position set for 'chiming,' the boys go up a ways just for fun." He smiled. "Like this."

He walked over to one of the ropes, seized the handgrip, and pulled down hard. As the rope went up Mr. Howard was lifted, perhaps six feet. Then as the rope descended, so did Mr. Howard, landing gracefully back on his feet.

A few Sundays later I returned to Kent and climbed up the belfry while the boys of the Bell Ringers Guild did change ringing on a peal of six bells. It's a little hard to describe the feeling you get; the boys in their Sunday suits minus jackets, looking exactly like photographs of English bell-ringers of the nineteenth century. The same rapt expressions on their faces; sweat pouring off them despite the open windows, freezing weather, and snow falling outside; the great bell booming and humming; the treble bells cascading notes out over the hills, dropping Christmas wreaths of sound over the Housatonic River and the school standing on its bank. And the ever changing sequences of the bells, sad one minute, gay the next.

There is an excitement about being in the midst of this, so close to the bells themselves, an elation that made me understand the mad, acrobatic bell-ringers of Seville, whom you will meet later.

When the change ringing was finished, the boys fought the bells, quite literally, so they would swing slower and slower and finally stop in the normal down position of a church bell. The boys wanted to practice Christmas carols, using the bells as chimes. This is done by pulling a different set of very thin ropes set in a panel on the wall; these are connected to hammers that strike the now stationary bells on the inside of the lip.

"Come on over," said Mr. Howard. "I'd like to have you get the feel of the tenor, the one I usually ring. She's down," he said. "You'll be all right."

I went over to the rope, seized the grip, and pulled. This was the big bell. There were 2,750 pounds of it over us, ready to spring to life. It moved. The grip went down a little as it began to swing, then up, down further, up fast, down still further, I felt a tingle all over me. I had made it do that! What a wonderful feeling! The grip started rushing up. I hung onto it with both hands as it rose, and up into the air I went with it.

"Hey!" yelled Mr. Howard.

When I came down, Mr. Howard and David Bailey, chairman of the Guild, put their arms around me to add their weight to mine so there would be no question of my taking off again.

I had read about bells having lives of their own in the minds of superstitious folk of other centuries. Of *course* they have! I know "my" bell seemed to come alive the moment I began to pull on the rope. Sheer weight and momentum give a bell an existence of its own. When the momentum is lost, it dies.

# 5
# Change Ringers

Change ringers have remained the same throughout the ages, except for a greatly modified thirst. Present-day groups whose societies began in the 1400's have inherited a strange and rich remembrance.

Change ringers were colorful. Even the names of their groups, which were more like athletic clubs than intellectual societies, were colorful.

I have a picture of the Ancient Society of College Youths that was taken in 1907. There are twelve men in it. At a guess, only one of the College Youths is under forty, three of them must be at least fifty, and one is in his sixties. But this name was typical. There were also the Bromley Youths, the Croyden Youths, the Cumberland Youths, the Surrey Youths, and so on. The Western Green Caps sound sporty, but more realistic is the name of another group of ringers known simply as The Leatherhead.

At one period in England their competitions were as avidly followed as today's cricket and soccer matches. Quite

_____ 1827 _____

When I am filled with liquor strong.
 Each man must drink & then ding-dong.
Drink not too much to Cloud your Knobbs
 Lest you forget to make the bobbs!
 --- a Gift of
 John Pattman, Beccles.

a few of the ancient societies are still in existence; their membership still maintains big-league status in the "sport," for that is exactly what they consider change ringing to be. Strangely enough, although their performances took place in a church, as a group they did not necessarily have a religious affiliation with any church. They were occasionally paid performers, and they were always given the run of the belfry for practice whenever they wished.

In the latter part of the eighteenth century and in the early decades of the nineteenth, the change ringers were a lively group. Frequently the prizes for their contests were liquid. In fact, it was traditional that a part of the ringers' pay was a gallon jug kept filled during working hours. The "ringers' jugs," or "jacks," as they are often called, have some antique value. A number of these jugs have been moved from churches to museums. Made of leather, metal, and earthenware, their inscriptions describe the bell-ringer of the day or at least indicate his thirst.

One pitcher preserved at Hinderclay, in Suffolk, bears the inscription:

> From London I was sent,
> As plainly doth appear
> it was to this intent—
> to be filled with strong beer.
> Pray to remember the pitcher when empty.

Perhaps the prize indication of the ringers' chronic thirst is the inscription on a bell dated 1702 that hangs at Walsgrave in Warwickshire:

HARKEN DO YE HEARE      OVR CLAPERES WANT BEERE

The fact that the spirited sportsmen of those days were not in the least slowed down by the amount of beer and ale they drank is borne out by a verse written by the parish clerk of St. Peter's Church in Norfolk. He lived near the church where the change ringers were in the habit of practicing at six on Sunday mornings. One day he reached the point where, so far as bells were concerned, he was finished. He wrote:

Ye rascally ringers, inveterate foes,
Disturbers of those who are fond of repose.
I wish, for the peace and the quiet of these lands
That ye had round your necks what ye pull with your hands.

Sadly for this man the time of "dumb practice" had not yet arrived when change ringers exercised on mute bells.

The rich days of the great change ringers have gone, but their independent attitude remains to this day one of their inherent characteristics. At Kent School we have a good example. The peal of ten bells was presented to that school in 1931 by Frank Humphreys and his wife. The bells were cast in England and were first rung in 1932. They belong to the school; but the students' Bell Ringers Guild of Kent, under the aegis of its faculty advisor, Mr. Howard, has full charge of their ringing.

On my first visit to the school I asked Mr. Howard when the guild would next be ringing. He said they usually rang from ten thirty until quarter of eleven Sunday mornings as well as sometimes in the late afternoon. I questioned him as to what afternoons. He answered that nobody knew, for it was entirely up to the boys; but that he might be able to find out a little ahead of time some day because he occasionally rang that big tenor bell in the peal band with them. I gather he was allowed to ring the bell by special permission, for he is one of the administrative executives of the school.

The most interesting thing he told me about this guild was that for one year after the bells were installed, there was a professional ringer at the school; but since then—for over thirty years now—the boys have handled the entire program themselves. The lore and the learning and the teaching has been handed down from class to class and from generation to generation. To me, this is fine and just how it should be, with anything so splendidly ancient.

There are very few active peals in this country. The most skillfully used is the new peal of ten bells at Groton School in Massachusetts. Change ringing is taken seriously at Groton. Russell Young, the ringing master, went to England to study the art before moving into the post; each year a group of Groton bell-ringers follow his path to the home of ringing. A second active peal is at Kent. At Ann Arbor, Michigan, there is a peal that I understand has not been used in years. (They favor hand-bell choirs at the university, and their "Spartan Bell Ringers" are regarded as just about the best.) There is also a peal at the Perkins Institute for the Blind in Boston, and sometimes it is rung by the "Grotties" and by the boys from Kent. Very recently a splendid new peal has been installed in the Episcopal Cathedral in Washington, D.C.

Our oldest change-ringing peal is as American as the thirteen colonies, yet so traveled as to be almost international. The bells hang now where they have hung always—well almost always—in the bell tower of St. Michael's Episcopal Church in Charleston, South Carolina. They are a change-ringing peal, no longer rung by hand but by the verdonic system.*

The bells of St. Michael's were hung in the mid-seventeen hundreds and were immediately called "the voice of

* The I. T. Verdin Company of Cincinnati, who imports cast bells from Petit and Fritzen, Founders, in Holland, coined the word *verdonic* in keeping with their competitor, Schulmerich, who had coined *carillonic*. The Verdin Company is what you might call "everyman's sexton," for they make electric timers and ringing mechanisms that can be placed on any existing bell to make it ring the hours or just about anything else you want.

Charleston." One black April night the signal lanterns were hung in the North Church in Boston and the countryside flamed into war.

In Charleston an English major stole the beautiful peal of bells from St. Michael's tower. The modern phrase would be "he liberated them," for he shipped them to England. There he sold them for private profit. It is doubtful whether he cared that by a small miracle he had actually sold the bells to a man who had formerly been a merchant in Charleston, who knew the bells and loved them so much he took care of them until the war's end and shipped them back to St. Michael's Church!

Once again the bells pealed the hours. Once again their notes were as much a part of the city of Charleston as the splashing of waves against the sea wall.

Then America was back at war with England, and this time the vestry of St. Michael's decided to move the bells to a remote church in Columbia, South Carolina. But alas this town, the church—and the bells—were burned by the British. What was to be done? Since the Revolution the British had proved themselves to be gentlemen and sportsmen, so the people of Charleston gathered the remains of their treasured bells and shipped them to England! There they were recast by the late enemy at the White Chapel Foundry, the same foundry that had cast the Liberty Bell.

Perhaps that's why the treble bells of that particular peal seem to have in them notes of laughter. Why not? They've crossed the ocean five times.

When Richard Fell, rector of St. Michael's, made a tape recording of his bells for a commemorative Independence Day record, he told me that the bells of St. Michael's had rung every Fourth of July since the first one (at least when they weren't in the hands of the British). He suggested that for the recording they might play the tunes and chimings they have always played on the Fourth. I said that was fine; then Mr. Fell, just a little hesitantly, added, "Perhaps I'd better explain to you that one of the tunes we play is not exactly what you might expect. You see, close to a century ago, the

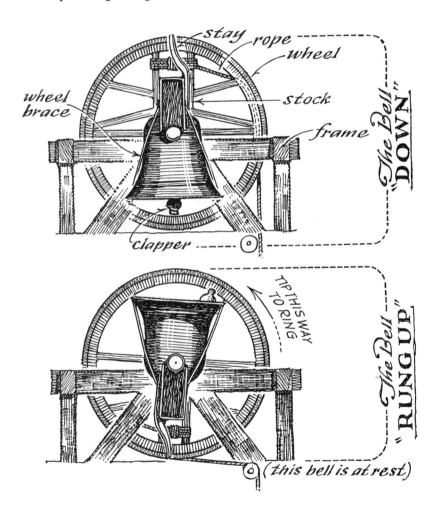

35

Fourth of July caught us with no bell-ringer except an ancient Negro who sometimes rang for the services. Well, of course he had to play a tune and this turned out to be the only one he knew."

I visualized a Negro spiritual, which I thought would sound wonderful on the bells. When I asked its name, Mr. Fell, who seemed to be stifling laughter, said, "I told you now, it is a little different. It's a tune called, 'Go Tell Aunt Nancy the Old Gray Goose Is Dead'!"

And that's how traditions are born.

Not to be neglected is the growing popularity of hand-bell ringing. Not too many years ago, there was little of this. Now, most fortunately, there are more than five hundred hand-bell choirs, composed of from eight to twenty-nine ringers, scattered throughout the country.

It is odd that there is so little change ringing in America, since the sound of bells has been so much a part of the American scene. But now it is the carillon that has captured our imagination. Could this be part of the laziness of our time? Gaining the greatest pleasure from the music of changes takes real knowledge and painstaking attention; while listening to a carillon takes no more effort than listening to the song of a lark.

# 6
## Carillons and Carillonics

The carillon came into being long ago, but where and how it began is any carillonneur's guess. It might have started with an ancient Chinese musical instrument, the "Pien Ching," consisting of sixteen stones which when hammered give off metallic tones and cover two octaves of notes. In China, however, octaves are somewhat different, for they contain those curious little quarter and half tones.

I very briefly described a carillon some pages back as a set of bells tuned to the intervals of the chromatic scale. To be recognized technically as a carillon, however, its range must encompass at least three octaves. The bell with the deepest note is the heaviest, and it is sometimes very heavy indeed. The Bourdon Bell in the carillon of Riverside Church in New York weighs 20½ tons and is the biggest tuned bell in the world. (Incidentally, this and several of the other large bells at Riverside are not stationary but, despite their vast size, are swung like church bells, with a power assist.) The bell of the highest note weighs nine pounds. Between these two there are seventy others of varying weights.

Carillons are played by hand but they are also, and have been for hundreds of years, played by mechanisms attached to clocks. These, like the drums in old-fashioned music boxes, trip little hammers, causing them to strike the outside of the bells. Though the selections are changed from time to time, the music, like all mechanically produced music, lacks the touch and feeling of the master musician's heart and hands.

The cast bell carillon in the form we know it today, has been with us for over four hundred years. It arrived at this state of near perfection in Belgium and Holland, for the sober and stolid Flemish, Belgians, and Dutch adopted the carillon as their own. There was a carillon in Dunkerque in 1437, one in Alost in 1487, and a huge carillon of sixty bells in the cathredal at Antwerp by 1540.

Why should it have been in these unlikely lowlands that the carillon came into its own? The name itself comes from the Laten *quadrilionem* and the Italian *quadriglio*—both of which are related to four-beat dances—and becomes, in French, *carillon*. In each of these the name is based on the word for *four* and possibly was used because the very earliest carillons (the word refers to the music as well as the instrument) were played on four bells.

My research has found no definitive explanation as to why

the carillons flourished in the lowlands. So I have formed a theory of my own. As sound travels better over plains and water than over hilly terrain, the carillon was perfectly suited to the low countries' flat land and abundant water—

particularly abundant when the dykes broke and there didn't happen to be a small Dutch boy present to put his finger in the hole.

A carillonneur sits in a room below the bells or in a room in the center of the carillon. The tiers of smaller bells are above him and the big deeper ones beneath. He plays his bells by striking wooden levers with the sides of his hands while sounding the deeper throated bells with foot pedals.

There is a fascinating description by the Rev. H. R. Haweis, which appeared in the *Magazine of Art* in 1882, of Monsieur J. Denyn, of Mechlin, one of the great carillonneurs, at work. It sounds more like a description of an athletic event than an account of a man making sweet music:

> I stood first at a remote corner of the Market-place. . . . and after a short running prelude from the top bells weighing only a few pounds to the bottom one of several tons, M. Denyn settled to his work at a brisk gallop, and ably sustained at a good tearing pace without flagging for a single bar. Such an effort, involving the most violent muscular exercise, could not last long as I quickly perceived when I entered the belfry and watched the player.

Mr. Haweis himself must have been quite an athlete, for he speaks casually of entering the belfry while Denyn was still going at that gallop; yet Mr. Haweis fails to mention that to get from the street to the belfry at Mechlin, he had to climb four hundred steps!

> He [Denyn] was bathed in sweat and every muscle of his body seemed at full tension, as with feet he grappled with the huge pedal bells and manipulated with gloved hands and incredible rapidity his two rows of key pegs. After a brief breathing pause . . . [he] gave me an astonishing specimen of bravura playing, putting down the great nine-ton and six-ton bells for the melody with his feet, and carrying on a rattling accompaniment of demi-quavers and demi-semi-quavers on the treble bells, and, finally, after a few sweeping arpeggios he broke into a processional movement so stately it reminded me of Chopin's *Funeral March*. Just after this when he was in the middle of a grand fantasia on the *Dame*

*Blanche* the clock barrel began working at the hour with a pretty French tune: *"Comme on aime a vingt ans."*

A lesser artist would have been taken aback! But M. Denyn seized his opportunity, and, waiting patiently until the barrel had done, plunged rapidly into an extempore continuation, which was so finely joined onto the mechanical tune that the people in the market-place must have thought that the barrel had suddenly become inspired. . . . then . . . as a tribute to (me) his English guest, he wound up with "God Save the Queen!"

Today many carillonneurs insist on total privacy when they are at the clavier. This is not temperament, but rather modesty. The work is so very strenuous they strip to their shorts to play. I can understand this; I tried playing a twenty-five-bell carillon recently and found that the force of the blows required to produce sounds from the bells was far greater than I had thought. I also found that after playing several bars of a hymn my hands ached, and I had had enough. In time, of course, carillonneurs develop protective calluses. But for hands too sensitive, it is possible to play with a glove.

Since the first quarter of this century the carillon of cast bells has become less a rarity in the United States. In 1930 there were only fifteen cast-bell carillons in this country while in Belgium and the Netherlands there were over a hundred. Now, though the wars have destroyed many of the bells in these countries, the number in North America has grown to more than a hundred.

Though the great carillon with its huge weight of bells will always be the true love of the carillonneur, during the past fifteen years there has been a good deal of electronic infidelity; and there is likely to be more of it. The infidelity

41

runs from the North American College in Vatican City to
St. Theresa Church in Fresno, California. This is not only
understandable but forgivable, as cast-bell carillons cost over
$100,000.

*Blessing the bells....*

*...Twentieth century.*

To describe just what constitutes a "carillonic bell," there
is this explanation from a pamphlet by Schulmerich Carillon
of Sellerseville, Pennsylvania, who coined the phrase.

> The "Arlington" Carillon uses precision-tuned, bell-
> metal *tone generators*, struck by metal hammers, as its tone
> sources.... Thus, because its action duplicates that of a
> metal clapper striking a cast bronze bell, the tones are pro-
> duced in the traditional manner.
>
> Through the magic of modern electronics, the faint but
> perfect vibrations of the bells of the "Arlington" Carillon
> are amplified millions of times and projected from the
> tower or roof by special stentors. [Stentors are simply
> loud-speakers.]

Somewhere between the cast giants with their pure voices and the midgets with their amplified ones, we have a third modern carillon. This is the Van Bergen Maas-Rowe Carillon, part of whose trademark is: "They sound like bells because they are bells." Well, they are. The Van Bergen Bell Foundry in Holland has been casting huge, beautiful bells for a long time. One of their bells, weighing 12,980 pounds, is in the carillon given to the American people by the people of the Netherlands. This is a magnificent instrument. The same Van Bergen Foundry casts the bells for their electronic carillons, but these bells are small. In fact, they have shrunk to the point where an entire carillon of thirty-seven or more bronze bells, "... occupies about the space of an upright piano ..." The sound is then electronically amplified.

Some people say, and the companies of course agree, that it is almost impossible for even an expert carillonneur to notice the difference between a cast-bell, full-scale carillon and an electronic one. Other persons claim the difference is plainly noticeable. The actual difference would seem to rest in the fact that cast bells with their thousands of pounds of vibrating metal produce concussion and that electronic reproductions of bells do not. I believe the difference *is* noticeable, particularly in the deep-throated notes—the BONG rather than the dong. One tends almost to feel rather than to hear the difference.

To counter the claim that electronic carillons do not create concussion, John Dougherty, vice-president of Schulmerich, tells this story.

A few years ago a famous conductor came to him and explained that he was going to conduct the Boston Symphony in the *1812 Overture* and that the sound of the three bells called for in the score had never been properly used because the composer had written notes for the bells that were at least two octaves below the possible range of any bell that had ever been made. He wanted to know if Schulmeric with their little rods and hammers and amplifiers could possibly produce these sounds. Without hesitation John said they could.

The afternoon of the concert Dougherty arrived at the auditorium in Boston with a set of stentors and an enclosed console with three buttons on it. He set the console on the stage and hung the speakers so they faced the auditorium. The conductor looked at this box with disgust, shrugged his shoulders, and said, "Ah, well, I'll signal the musicians to play very softly so your little sounds can be heard."

"Perhaps," said John, "you'd like to hear them?"

The maestro shrugged, the muscians stared, and Dougherty pushed the buttons. The maestro and musicians jumped; it was immediately obvious that even if the symphony orchestra played its loudest, they were the ones who would not be heard. Furthermore, the stage hands had to spend the rest of the afternoon stuffing padding in all the auditorium windows that had been shaken loose by the deep vibrations.

Schulmerich, the Verdin Company, Van Bergen, and others, have installed between ten and fifteen thousand electronic carillons of various sizes all over the world. Considering these instruments cost only a fraction of the full-scale, cast-bell type, this means that the lovely, majestic music of beautiful bells has been brought to *millions* of people who might never have had their lives brightened by its enjoyment.

Can the carillonneurs be blamed for faithlessness to their first loves when they have had a part in doing this? Ah, no!

For the big bells will always be there, too, booming, throbbing, and sending chills of thrilled excitement out through their vibrant voices.

These voices, however, are not always as harmonious as they might be. In fact, at times they can be extremely raucous. The big bells in Spain are a good example, and the Giralda Tower in Seville is typical. The accepted ringing method is done by a rope attached to a tremendous timber lever. This is fastened to the center of the stock and, protruding upward, acts as a counterweight to the bell itself. As the bells are rung, they swing over and the rope winds around the stock. In "normal" ringing, this round-and-round business gradually retards the motion of the bell until it can be held up on end. These bells are generally hung in the wide-open arches of square towers, and first the bell and then the timber lever on top of it swing clear of the tower and out over the landscape. Now let Mr. Gadow, author of the book *Northern Spain*, describe what goes on in Seville's Giralda Tower:

> There are a dozen great bells which send forth the most discordant and unceasing peals, and the ringing of them is a strange exhibition. They are swung round and round; the rope is allowed to coil itself round the stock, or is jerked on the lip of the bell, and the ringer springs up by staunchions on the wall to get a purchase, then throws himself down; or he allows himself to be carried by the rope as it swings round outside. As I entered the gallery, I saw one of the ringers thrown out, as I imagined and expected, of course, that he would be dashed on the pavement below. I saw him the next moment perched on [top of] the bell, smiling at my terror.

45

At San Salvador young boys, for a fee, execute a similar performance. When the rope gets all wound up and the bell is ringing quite slowly, they leap onto the lever attached to the stock and ride over the bell and out through the arch. Then quickly moving in toward the stock, they stop the bell and by balancing hold it stationary at right angles to the ground far below them. When urged to start ringing again they step back toward the stock and, as the bell swings over itself bringing them back into the bell chamber, they hop off and just let her ring until the rope is unwound.

Thus from ancient China to twentieth-century Spain, carillons and carillonics have developed their own variations and their own methods of performance.

Giralda Tower.

# 7
# Sounds and Legends!

In all my research I have found nothing definitive on how far the sound of bells will carry. Under different weather conditions the peal will transmit varying distances. Cold and still air is an effective carrier; warm and moving air is not.

I decided to get a bell and carry out a test. Borrowing a ship's bell from a friend, I stood outside my house one night and persuaded my wife to drive down the road, stopping periodically to see if she could still hear me ringing. She was able to hear me for a distance of exactly half a mile.

From this experiment I presumed to have learned that a bronze bell 7½ inches wide at the lip, 6 inches high, and weighing 4 pounds rung at an altitude of 1,200 feet above sea level can be heard for a distance of 2,640 feet. Here was a formula for figuring the distance any bell would carry if

I knew its size and weight. When I tried to apply this formula to the bell whose sound had carried from London to Windsor, a distance of twenty miles, my formula said it should have carried an additional 2,400 hundred miles. Hence, I gave up my formula and the idea of ever finding one.

While sound is temporal, legends endure. For a legend is simply a story that has passed down through the ages. Among legends relating to bells, some are macabre and some are humorous.

There was once an emperor who ordered a great bell to be cast and he entrusted the work to a mandarin named Kuan-yu. Over and over again Kuan-yu's castings failed; and finally the emperor sent word to him that if one more failure occurred, there would be a swishing sound followed by a swift crunch, then a plop, and that the plop would be the sound of Kuan-yu's head hitting the ground. Like all legendary mandarins, this one had a beautiful daughter. Her name was Ko-ai. As she was an unusually devoted daughter, she went to see a clairvoyant priest and asked, "How can I save my father?"

After several astrological observations, the priest told her that the only way to insure a perfect bell-casting was to see to it that the blood of a pure maiden was mixed with the molten metal.

Ko-ai went at once to the place where the bell was about to be cast, and crying, "For my father!" she flung herself into the huge, seething vat of liquid bronze. The casters tried to rescue her, but it was impossible. When the outer mold was stripped away and the bell was hung, the casting turned out to be perfect; but Kuan-yu had ceased to care. The great bell was rung. Its tone was perfection, but, to the horror of the thousands assembled to hear its voice, the deep resonance of its first sounding was followed by a strange high note, a very human wail.

To return to how far the sound of a bell will carry, there is this dubious but somewhat more cheerful legend. A long time ago in Toledo, Spain, a young man killed his opponent in a duel. Becaused this particular instance of polite murder was frowned on by the authorities, he fled to the cathedral for safety. His father, who was a rich count and famed bell fancier, went to the King to fix things up. The King did go so far in whimsicality as to say that if the count could make a bell in Toledo that could be heard all the way to the palace in Madrid, his son would be pardoned.

The count did this, and the son was quickly pardoned. The distance from Toledo to Madrid is sixty miles.

Another and very possibly true anecdote is about a bell, "Great Tom of Westminster," and a soldier on sentry duty at Windsor Castle during the reign of William III.

The sentry was accused of sleeping at his post. When formally charged with this most serious of offenses, he said to his superior, "I was not asleep, Sir, for I heard Great Tom strike at midnight."

"A likely story!" said the officer. "Westminster is full twenty miles from here."

"But, Sir, I did. I had special reason to remember it."

"And what reason?"

"Because, Sir, Great Tom struck thirteen times."

On occasion since then Great Tom actually has struck thirteen times, and it may well have done so on that particular night. After 1698, the bell was removed from its tower, recast, and hung in St. Paul's of London, where, shortly after that, it cracked and has since rung only to strike the hour and to toll at the funerals of royalty and other personages of great estate.

There is another legend of bell sounds that involves a valley in Nottinghamshire said to have been formed by a terrible earthquake many centuries ago. One Christmas morning, while the bells were tolling, a whole village was plunged beneath the earth. Every Christmas thereafter, so the story goes, if you put your ear to the ground you can hear the bells tolling again. What people have actually heard, however, are the bells from the church in a village a few miles away.

It's incredible but true that in 1793 the parishioners of Newington Church in England sold their church bells in order to raise the money to build a steeple in which to hang them!

In the fifteenth century a man, known only as Christian, was engaged to cast a bell to be hung in the south tower of the church of St. Mary Magdalene in Breslau. He was a gray-faced man better known for his quick temper than for his artistry as a bell-founder.

After weeks of work the core and cope were made, and the finest bell metal was procured and cast into the forge as the fires were brought to white heat. Just then a messenger arrived at Christian's house. Judging from the pounding at the door that it must be something important, the founder went into his house to answer the knock. Before he left, he told his young helper not to touch anything, mold or furnace, on pain of death, as the critical moment when he would pour was almost at hand.

Christian had hardly left when the boy, alone in the huge, dark room with the mold and the furnace, became possessed by an uncontrollable impulse to touch and see what would happen. He touched the metal catch that held the door of the forge closed, then leaped back in terror. With a roar and a hiss a river of glowing, molten metal poured from the furnace. The dark founding room became murky with steam. The boy ran screaming for his master just as Christian came back into the foundry and saw what to him was his own life's blood streaming wasted across the brick floor toward the pit where the mold of the bell lay. In a flash of blinding rage, he struck out with all his might. The boy fell dead.

What made his maddened action unbearable to Christian was that even as he killed the boy, the metal ran into the mold, filling it to the top. And days later, when the cope was removed and the bell lifted from the pit, it was smooth and beautiful in line, curve, and finish. With block, chain, and tackle he raised the bell clear of the cope. Its beauty enraged him and made the boy's death obscene. He seized a hammer, hoping to shatter the bell. Before the blow could land, a note sweeter and purer than any he had ever heard came from the swaying bell. Somehow he knew, though the tone came from the bell, it was not the bell he was hearing but instead was the voice of the boy whose soul had flowed with the metal.

He flung his hammer away and dropped to his knees in prayer, asking forgiveness and guidance. After a long while he rose, knowing what he must do. He left the foundry and marched to the house of the high sheriff to confess. Shortly thereafter he was hanged. The first time the new bell was rung from St. Mary's briefly, it tolled the funeral of the angry man who had created it. The bell was dedicated as "St. Mary's Bell." But it is still known, almost six hundred years later, as "The Bell of the Poor Sinner."

# 8

## Inscriptions on Bells

Once you could tell who manufactured anything by just looking at it; as the saying goes, the maker's personality was "written all over it." And bells were no exception.

As soon as a craftsman was finished designing some piece of work he was proud of, he felt compelled to include upon it a date, his initials, and often just anything that popped into his head. Take the inscription on this old bell:

ARISE AND GO TO YOUR BUSINESS

which probably represents the absolute nadir of inscription writing. The level is raised only slightly in this one:

I RING AT SIX TO LET MEN KNOW WHEN TO
AND FROM THEIR WORK TO GO

And still in the pedantic vein, but again a little better, this one from a founder who believed in hedging his bets:

OUR VOICES SHALL IN CONCERT RING TO
HONOR BOTH OF GOD AND KING

One from a man who obviously had little faith in his craftsmanship:

IF YOU HAVE A JUDICIOUS EAR
YOU'LL OWN MY VOICE IS SWEET AND CLEAR

There is a strong tendency to use the first-person singular or plural in all bell inscriptions. This is the result of a curious psychotic reaction that runs through all literature about bells. Reference is made to them not as to so many hundreds of pounds of metal or even as musical instruments but as living, independent entities capable of expressing emotions of their own. Thus Tennyson speaks of them as "Wild bells" and Poe refers to wedding bells as "Ringing out their delight."

Bells, in other words, are taken seriously. Even when their inscriptions are tongue-in-cheek, like this:

ALL YE OF BATH WHO HEAR ME SOUND
THANK LADY HOPTON'S HUNDRED POUND

These inscriptions, despite their levity, apparently did not in the least daunt the strait-laced clergy of the day, for there is hardly an ancient church bell anywhere whose installation and hanging was not accompanied by a christening of the bells. In some cases, this was baptismal. In all cases, consecration ceremonies were conducted by the vicar, rector, or even the bishop, as the importance of the bells demanded.

Church bells sometimes announced "a sermon will be heard

at prayer services today." Such a bell hanging at Blakesley in Northants, England, was inscribed:

I RING TO SERMON WITH A LUSTY BOME,
THAT ALL MAY COME AND NONE MAY STOP AT HOME

The Puritans who enjoyed preaching so much they often stayed away from church unless there was to be a sermon, became a problem to one Bishop Wren. So in 1640 he ordered church bells to ring just the same whether there was to be a sermon or not.

People collect bell inscriptions as they do gravestone markings. The following are samples:

GIFTS FREE BOUGHT MEE
(Pilton, Somerset, 1726)

ONCE I'D A NOTE THAT NONE COULD BEAR
BUT BILBIE MADE ME SWEET AND CLEAR
(Bilbie Foundry, 1798)

I MEAN TO MAKE IT UNDERSTOOD
THAT THOUGH I'M LITTLE YET I'M GOOD
(Treble Bell at All-Saints)

THE GIFT OF JOS. PIZZIE AND WM. GWYNN
MUSIC & RINGING WE LIKE SO WELL
AND FOR THAT REASON WE GAVE THIS BELL
(Aldbourne, Wilts., 1787)

WHEN BACKWARDS RUNG WE TELL OF FIRE
THINK HOW THE WORLD SHALL THUS EXPIRE
(St. Ives, 1790)

IT IS REMARKABLE THAT THESE BELLS WERE
MOULDED DURING THE GREAT FROST
(York, 1783)

CURSED BE ALL CHURCH ROBBERS
(Norfolk, 1622)

THIS OLD BELL RUNG THE DOWNFALL OF
BUONAPARTE AND BROKE APRIL 1814
(Ashover, Derbyshire)

One founder evidentally at a loss for a suitable inscription, for a bell at Geddington, Northants, says:

ABCDEF                GHIKLM                NOPQRS

Very often the inscriptions on bells are just *there*, for no reason one can figure out. There is a case of this in East-hampton, Connecticut—"Jingletown"—where Bevins Broth-

*Jingletown (U.S.A.) bells*

ers have for many years made bells by the ton and sold them by the pound, and still do. (A manufactured bell, incidentally, sells for about $2.50 a pound.) I drove up there one winter's day and talked with Chauncey Bevins and Avery West. Their catalogue had shown a set of cast cowbells ranging in size from a couple of inches in diameter for calflets

The Swiss Cow-Bell that predated itself.

to 7½ inches for mammas. The bells were called Musical Swiss Cowbells, and they bore the inscription "Saignelegier," in script, and then above this in old-fashioned numerals, "1878." I was curious; I couldn't for the life of me figure out why they would put that particular date on bells cast in 1963.

The Bevins Brothers bell foundry was built in 1832. When I saw *that* inscription over the doorway in the old rose-brick office building, I was disappointed. *Why* couldn't it have said 1878?

Mr. West and Mr. Bevins greeted me at the door. After a brief hello, I immediately raised the question that had been on my mind: "Why do you have bells made in 1963 that say 1878 on them?"

Amused, Mr. Bevins replied: "I've seen some of our very old Swiss cowbells stamped 1865, 1866, and so on—right up to 1878. When the year 1879 came, the foundry probably got an unexpected rush order for sets of these bells, and they'd lost nine."

"Nine what?" I asked him.

"Not what," said Mr. Bevins. "Just plain nine. They'd lost the number nine. So they went on using eight."

Then we went for a tour of the factory, where they do everything from casting bells on exactly the same principle used four thousand years ago to turning out replicas of the Town Crier's bell similar to the one I rang on the Fourth of July. Bevins Brothers make about a million bells a year. The only other product they make is a brass knob that screws onto the horn of an ox!

# 9
## Founders and Foundries

It is very strange that an nation like ours, which has done so much to advance and improve on the nature of almost anything that can be manufactured, has over the centuries done so little about making bigger and better bells. There never were a great many bell-founders in this country who cast bells of any great size.

Of nine notable American firms,* only the McShane Bell Foundry Company in Baltimore and Bevins Brothers in East-hampton, Connecticut are left. Though McShane will accept orders for bells of up to ten thousand pounds, Bevins will not cast a bell over ten inches in diameter. In addition to the nine original firms, there were two men whose names have become

---

* A complete list of the nine notable early American bell-founders appears in the Appendix.

famous, Pass and Stow of Philadelphia. These two recast the Liberty Bell when it cracked in 1753, though the official Independence Hall account of the incident does not refer to them as foundrymen, merely noting that the bell "...was recast by two workmen, Pass and Stow."

A great deal of the early bell-casting was done by individuals rather than by foundries. Probably, however, most of these individuals had much more experience in the art than the two famous Philadelphians. Furthermore, the habit of the times was not to cast big bells at one central place, but to set up temporary foundries in convenient places and there cast such bells as were ordered by churches in neighboring districts. A still more practical method frequently practiced in the fifteen and sixteen hundreds, when the English roads left a great deal to be desired, was casting big bells in the yards of the churches where they were to hang. Remains of furnaces discovered during excavations in such places as the open court of the church at Scalford in Leicestershire and at Epingham in Rutland attest to this practice. And it is well known that when in 1762 the great bell of Canterbury Cathedral was lowered to the ground for recasting, the founding was done in the cathedral yard.

Bell-casting in England became an established industry at an early age; so well established, in fact, that in 1483 importing foreign bells was declared illegal as it was reducing domestic profits. There were many bell-founders in England, and unlike our American bell foundries, many of them have survived. A letter I received recently from Douglas Hughes, a partner of the Whitechapel Bell Foundry in London, illustrates the longevity of British bell-founders. The letterhead contains the phrase "Established 1570." The letter itself speaks with interest about our American Fourth of July bell-ringing ceremonies and goes on to mention that this foundry, which cast the Liberty Bell in 1752, a number of years ago offered to recast it free of charge. They received indirect word from President Truman extending his deep appreciation for the offer but saying that the cracked Liberty Bell had become such an object of reverance to the American people that he wouldn't dare suggest its recasting.

I have the latest Whitechapel Foundry booklet at hand; it looks as though it might have been printed at any time within the last three hundred years. It includes a list of the twenty-eight chief founders since 1570, including the three Hughes men who are the partners today. This short statement from it I find appealing: "the eight bells at Westminster Abbey came from Whitechapel between 1583 and 1919, and we have recently rehung them; an unbroken connection [business] of over 350 years."

There is also a picture of an Ernest Oliver testing the pitch of a hand bell with a tuning fork and the modest sentence, "There have been members of the Oliver family at the Whitechapel Foundry for well over 200 years." Whitechapel still casts the majority of bells imported to this country today.

Among the most famous founders of all time is an American who is better known than any other bell-founder anywhere, though he is generally remembered for accomplishments other than bell-casting. As an express rider he once made the round trip to Philadelphia and back in nine days at a time when most riders took that long to ride it one way. As a colonel in the Continental Army he was a bit uninspired, regarding war as destructive rather than creative. But as a munitions-maker, a printer of currency, and a manufacturer of boilers, he was superb. He was a top American silversmith and designer, an artist, and an engineer. For all these remarkable abilities, his greatest fame comes from one ride on a horse.

The way Paul Revere got started in the bell-casting business is entirely typical of his, "Well, gentlemen, if I don't know how to do it I can sure as anything find out how pretty

quick" attitude toward everything in life. What happened was that the bell in Boston's Old North Church tower cracked in the year 1792. In almost any other year the logical thing would have been to ship the remains to England and have them recast. Understandably the directors of Paul Revere's church felt the English might feel just a little touchy about being asked to recast this particular bell.

It being a mechanical problem, the solution was simple. Get neighbor Paul to recast it. Paul went to work. He rode to Abington to talk with foundryman Aaron Hobart, and he came back with Hobart's foreman. He made his mold and cope and poured bell metal into the space between them. The long cooling period passed. Finally the bell emerged from the mold, and the great day came when the bell was hung and a clapper swung to produce the first silvery note.

It was a day still remembered in Boston, for the note that Paul Revere's first bell loosed into the world was beyond any doubt the worst note any bell-founder had yet achieved. It was conservatively described by a Bostonian of the time as "panny, harsh, and shrill." But to the Bostonians, it was beautiful. Their own Paul Revere had made it!

That was only the beginning. After he had sheathed the bottom of Old Ironsides with copper, Paul Revere really went at bell-casting. He studied and talked to people who knew bells.

Since copper represented such a large proportion of bell metal and American copper was far from plentiful and often of doubtful quality in America during the years of Revere's bell-casting, it is amazing that he achieved in his bells not only beauty but timelessness.

His masterpiece, his "great bell," was cast for Kings Chapel, Boston, in 1817. Today it still hangs in its belfry overlooking the heart of the city.

Not long ago I talked with Mr. Harold Haynes, verger of King's Chapel, to check on the condition of the bell and get the date on it, which I couldn't find in my research library. Mr. Haynes has a proper affection for things old and beautiful, and he spoke glowingly of the bell.

"The sweetest bell Paul Revere ever made. It says so right on the bell, 'The sweetest bell we ever made. Paul Revere & Son. 1817.'"

He told me the bell had originally been one of the Londonderry Chimes but that it had cracked in 1814 while tolling evening service. When Revere recast it, a lot of good Bostonians threw silver into the melting pot "to add more sweetness to the tone." I have an idea that Yankee frugality must

# CHURCH BELLS.

## PAUL REVERE & SON,

*No.* 13, *Lynn Street,* North End, BOSTON,

HAVE conſtantly for ſale, CHURCH and ACADEMY BELLS, of all ſizes, which they will warrant *equal* to any made in Europe, or this *country.* From perſonal information obtained in Europe, and twenty years experience, they are aſſured they can give ſatisfaction, and will ſell, on as good terms, as they can be imported for, or obtained in this country.

have been at work in this situation, for with a high percentage of silver the bell would have soured long before now.

Mr. Haynes went on. "I ring out the old year on her and I ring in the new and I ring her for all regular services and for anything special, like Lindbergh's landing in Paris. I rang that out on her, too."

Then he thanked me for getting in touch with him, adding that somehow none of the other people who wrote about the bell in books managed to get its weight correct.

The Paul Revere Bell at King's Chapel, Boston, weighs exactly 2,475 pounds, without the clapper, which weighs an additional fifteen pounds.

Of the four hundred odd bells Paul Revere's firm made, forty-eight of them were cast during his lifetime. Thanks to Dr. Arthur Nichols and the study he made of Revere bells in 1911 and to the published work of Edward C. and Evelyn Stickney, specialists in Paul Revere bells (from which work they have most graciously permitted me to use material), it would appear that roughly three hundred have been either sent out of the country, burned in church fires, or (believe it or not), simply mislaid. About one hundred can be accounted for.

Of the bells Paul Revere himself cast, thirty-seven are still in existence.* Perhaps a dozen of these, unspoiled by mishanging, bad ringing, or other abuse, still ring out the sweet sounds he created so long ago.

* A list of the thirty-seven bells cast by Paul Revere that are still in existence appears in the Appendix.

the *Liberty* Bell

Throughout history there have been bells that have rung, pealed, and tolled events of significance in the lives of many people. There is the Lutine Bell of Lloyds of London, at the Royal Exchange. This is a beautiful though small bell, mounted in an ornate filigree, with a most appropriate ship's anchor chain hung on it.

The bell first belonged to the *Lutine*, a French frigate. When the frigate was captured by an English ship, the bell changed homes. That English boat was wrecked at the entrance to the Zuider Zee in 1799, and Lloyds acquired the salvage rights to her; so the bell changed ownership again. It is still connected with the sea, for it is tolled with solemn majesty to announce the loss of any vessel insured by Lloyds.

A companion to this bell is the gong on the New York Stock Exchange. It is electric and roughly three feet in diameter. It clangs each morning at ten to announce the opening of the exchange and again at three to call the closing. But when this gong sounds just one stroke while the exchange is in session, a hush passed over the floor. It causes many a member to feel the chill of apprehension. For the sound of the one sonorous stroke means that a member firm has failed or has been expelled from membership, or that a member of the exchange has died. In the great depression of the thirties, the members became almost accustomed to the sound of the gong. An officer of the exchange told me a little diffidently that, for some reason he could not explain, the sound of the gong is different when it is rung to bespeak tragedy. I can understand.

Then there is the Liberty Bell in Philadelphia. It has its own mystique; for although the final casting took place in 1753, just short of a quarter of a century before the bell rang out the news of the proclamation of the Declaration of Independence in 1776, it bore the inscription:

PROCLAIM LIBERTY THROUGHOUT ALL THE LAND . . . AND
TO ALL THE INHABITANTS THEREOF.

The story is well known and only the bare facts need repeating. The bell cracked once and was recast, as mentioned earlier. Though it may have rung on the Fourth of July in '76, when the Continental Congress approved the Declaration of Independence, it *did* ring on July 8 to announce the proclamation of the Declaration.

The present crack in the bell occurred on the day in 1835 when it was being tolled in honor of John Marshall, chief justice of the United States Supreme Court, as his body passed through Philadelphia on the way to burial.

The bell presently stands in the entrance of Independence Hall in Philadelphia. It cannot be rung, and it would take a mighty cause to persuade its guardians even to tap it with a rubber hammer as was last done in World War II.

Strangely enough, the Liberty Bell has a "twin," cast by Whitechapel in London, of the same dimensions and within a few pounds of the same weight. This one was hung a year later in Christ Church at Second and Market Streets in Philadelphia, where it still hangs and still rings daily. It has never in all these long and turbulent decades shown the least sign of a crack.

I have wondered greatly about this and have at last come to believe that neither time, mishanging, nor misringing weakened the Liberty Bell, but rather the enormous import- ance of the message its voice cried out. It rang many strokes, loud and clear, but it rang only two words: "Liberty"— "FREEDOM!" And the ringing of them was to affect all mankind forevermore and to change the mighty course of history.

But let us remember what the Declaration of Independence meant to the men who signed it, what it has always meant to their countrymen. To quote from a contemporary account:

> On the Fourth of July in 1776, after a year of widely separated battles and skirmishes, in a desperate gesture to present a united effort in the struggle to win our freedom from the most blatant kind of tyranny and oppressions, a group of men met in the State House at Philadelphia [now Independence Hall]. There they, delegates from all

thirteen of the American colonies, officially known as the Continental Congress, signed and approved a document called the Declaration of Independence.

On that day we became a nation. On that day, too, we, a sparsely settled land of merchants, sailors, and farmers without adequate weapons, ammunition, or military supplies of any sort—including money; with our only weapons a few rifles and the enormous will and courage in our hearts, together with our faith in God, formally took on the whole and awesome might of the British Empire.

The men who signed Jefferson's document that long-ago summer in the State House in Philadelphia *knew* that if the war with England were lost this document they were signing would be of interest only because each would be signing his own death warrant. All would be hanged as traitors to the crown. It took extraordinary courage.

I have been thinking a lot about the Liberty Bell lately, and as a result of this I have come to a conclusion.

All my fierce calculating while I searched for a formula that would tell me the carrying range of a bell was time wasted. I was using the wrong kind of measurement. I have now learned that the voices of bells should not be measured in feet, yards, and miles, but should instead be measured in years, decades, and centuries. Here is my new and demonstrably correct equation:

One peal of a bell 4 feet in diameter, 3 feet in height, and weighing 2,080 lbs., hanging in Philadelphia, can be heard for a minimum of 187 years.

# Appendix

The nine notable early American bell-founders:

Hobart of Abington, Massachusetts
Fulton of Pittsburgh, Pennsylvania
Meneely Bros., of Troy, New York
Stukstede & Bros. of St. Louis, Missouri
William Blake & Co. of Troy, New York
Jones and Company of Troy, New York
The Buckeye Bell Foundry of Cincinnati, Ohio
Bevins Brothers of Easthampton, Connecticut
The McShane Bell Foundry Co., Inc. of Baltimore, Maryland

A list of the thirty-seven bells cast by Paul Revere that are still in existence:

1792, St. James Episcopal Church, N. Cambridge, Mass. Marked "The first church bell cast by P. Revere in Boston, 1792"

1795, Congregational Church, Groveland, Mass. Marked "Revere 1795, The living to the church I call, and to the grave I summon all"

1797, First Congregational Church, Essex, Mass. Marked "Revere & Sons Boston 1797"

1798, Historical Society, Dedham, Mass. Marked "Revere Boston 1798"

1801, First Parish Church, Weston, Mass. Marked "Paul Revere & Sons Boston 1801"

1801, Bentley School, Salem, Mass. Marked "Revere & Sons Boston 1801"

1802, New Old South Church, Worcester, Mass. Marked "Revere & Son Boston 1802"

1802, Congregational Church, Newington, N. H. Marked "Revere & Son Boston 1802"

1802, Town Hall, Milford, N. H. Marked "Revere & Son Boston 1802"

1803, Meetinghouse of the First Presbyterian Society, Old South, Newburyport, Mass. Marked "Revere & Son Boston 1803"

1804, M. T. Stevens & Sons Co., North Andover, Mass. Marked "Revere & Son Boston 1802"

1804, First Congregational Parish, Unitarian, Kennebunk, Me. Marked "Revere & Son Boston 1804"

1805, First Parish Church, Unitarian, East Bridgewater, Mass. Marked "Revere & Son Boston 1804"

1805, City Hall, Bath, Me. Marked "Revere & Son Boston 1802"

1806, The First Universalist Society in America, Gloucester, Mass. Marked "Revere & Son Boston 1806"

1807, Congregational Church, West Barnstable, Mass. Marked "Revere & Son Boston 1807"

1807, North Parish Church, North Andover, Mass. Marked "Revere & Son Boston 1806"

1807, Riverdale Methodist Church, Gloucester, Mass. Marked "Revere & Son Boston 1806"

1809, The Congregational Church, Northboro, Mass. Marked "Revere & Son Boston 1809"

1809, St. Paul's Church, Newburyport, Mass. Marked "Revere & Son Boston 1809"

1810, Congregational Parish, Unitarian, in Norton, Mass. Marked "Revere & Son Boston 1809"

1811, First Church, Congregational Meetinghouse, Hopkinton, N. H. Marked "Revere & Son Boston 1811"

1811, First Parish Church, Unitarian, Bridgewater, Mass. Marked "Revere & Son Boston 1811"

1811, First Parish Church, Needham, Mass. Marked "Revere & Son Boston 1811"

1814, The First Parish, Wayland, Mass. Marked "Revere & Son Boston 1814"

1815, First Congregational Church, Princeton, Mass. Marked "Revere & Son Boston 1815"

1815, Beebe Memorial Library, Wakefield, Mass. Marked "Revere & Son Boston 1815"

1816, Town Hall, North Hampton, N. H. Marked "Revere & Son Boston 1815"

1816, The First Church of Christ, Longmeadow, Mass. Marked "Revere & Son Boston 1815"

1816, King's Chapel, Boston, Mass. Marked "Revere & Son Boston 1816"

1816, First Congregational Church, Unitarian, Providence, R. I. Marked "For the Congregational Church, Providence, R. I., Revere & Son Boston 1816"

1816, First Methodist Church, Lynn, Mass. Marked "Revere & Son Boston 1816"

1816, Second Parish Church, Dorchester, Mass. Marked "Revere & Son Boston 1816"

1817, First Congregational Church, Norwich, Vt. Marked "Revere & Son Boston 1817"

1817, The Congregational Church of Topsfield, Mass. Marked "Revere & Son Boston 1817"

1818, St. Michael's Church, Marblehead, Mass. Marked "Revere & Son Boston 1818"

1818, The Congregational Church, Woodstock, Vt. Marked "Revere & Son Boston 1818"

# The Sound of Bells

Eric Sloane

# Contents

## Author's Note

If it were not for Independence Day, this book would not have been written, for the subject of bells does not immediately seem of much importance in the history of America. Yet a few years ago when I noticed the frequent mention of Independence Day bells in early diaries and eighteenth-century account books, I began to wonder. Back in 1957 when I wrote *The Seasons of America Past*, I first realized that bells had a special place in Americana.

"When Chinese firecrackers entered the scene," I wrote, "Independence Day bell-ringing vanished. But the thought of church bells and farm bells and school bells and fire bells all clanging through the countryside seems best to catch the spirit of that first great American day. It would be fitting, it seems, to revive the bells of Independence Day."

A few years later when my neighbor Eric Hatch joined with me to make my dream come true, President Kennedy made a proclamation, a resolution was passed in the U. S. Congress, and state proclamations were made urging that Independence Day be celebrated "this year and on every year following by the ringing of bells." Already there are small children who think this was always an uninterrupted custom; children who have never shot off a firecracker but who now look forward to ringing bells on July Fourth.

Now after more than four years of working on the Independence Day bell project, it seems that the revival has taken hold. The "bell room" where my wife, along with Eric Hatch and his wife, had kept office handling the ton or so of mail that poured in, has now become a bedroom again. And the next job seems to be that of getting bells to American children; for the bells can't be rung unless there are bells to be had.

So there you are with an explanation for this book, *The Sound of Bells*. I hope that it might not only enrich the lore of Americana, but also, and perhaps more important, that it might enrich the lives of many young Americans.

Eric Sloane
Weather Hill
Warren, Connecticut

# The Bells of Early America

The sounds of America were once good to hear. Not the unnerving noises of automobiles and vacuum cleaners and factory whistles and airplanes and sirens and the clatter of garbage pails and the screech of brakes and horns. Instead there was a comforting serenity.

In the winter there were the slithery squeals of sled runners and the soft clip-clop of horses' hoofs in the snow. There were also sleigh bells which made almost continuous winter music. In the summer the scissors grinder and rag picker and street vendor went from street to street calling out, and they were always ringing a handbell.

At night the stillness was often broken by the distant wail of the old-time steam locomotive; this could be sad or joyous or lonesome or adventurous, according to your own mood. But it was always music, never just noise. When the train whistle ceased, you could still hear the locomotive's bell which was big and clangorous, and it seemed to continue as if by habit, even when the train had come to a halt. As the drawing shows, the locomotive bell had a heavy counterbalance which helped keep it swinging back and forth.

As you approached any early American village, you would always hear the soft thump and splash of the old-time grist mill water wheels. What sounded like distant thunder usually turned out to be the hollow roar of some horse and wagon going through the wooden tunnel of a covered bridge. Even in the heart of town, if you listened carefully, you might hear the sounds of outlying farms, of cows and chickens and the constant tinkle of cow bells.

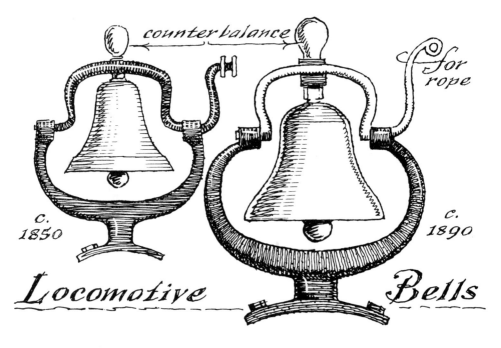

counterbalance

for rope

c. 1850

c. 1890

*Locomotive* *Bells*

At the end of day, when the big squat iron farm dinner bells began to sound, cows took it as a signal to wander in the direction of their barns, and all the sounds of the countryside began to quiet. But most commanding and carrying and respected was the voice of the great town bell and church bell. In their

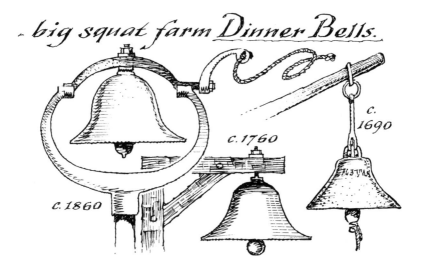

*big squat farm* Dinner Bells.

c. 1760

c. 1690

c. 1860

belfries, whenever their mouths opened to the countryside and the thunderous tones of bell sound floated over the surrounding hills, all the people listened.

At first, when meeting houses served both as town hall and place of worship, the building was simple, either square or round and without any belfry or steeple on top. A bell was either hung from a nearby tree or from a "bell pole," high enough to cast the sound of the bell over the rooftops and on to distant

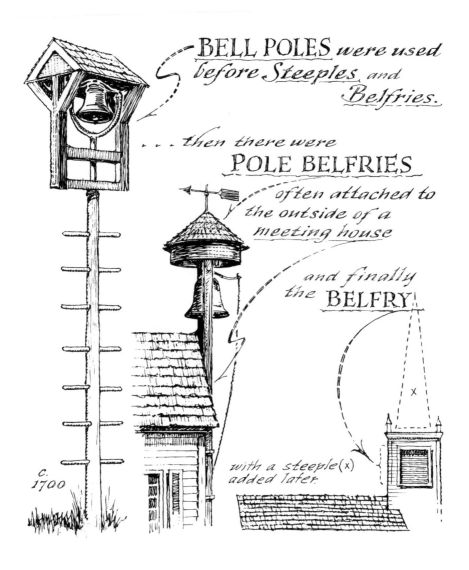

BELL POLES *were used before Steeples, and* Belfries.

....*then there were* POLE BELFRIES *often attached to the outside of a meeting house*

*and finally the* BELFRY

*with a steeple(x) added later*

c. 1700

farms. Later, there was a double poled bell, hanging with the bell swinging between the two poles, and this contraption was fastened directly to the building. Finally, of course, the bell was housed in a belfry as an actual part of the building and during later years a steeple was sometimes added on top of the belfry.

At first, these great bells did not call out the hour as they do nowadays, but they did sound three special hours of the day. At six in the morning there was a signal to remind everyone that day was already in progress and that all was well. It was time to begin work. At twelve there was a noon bell, the signal for lunching and that period known to the early farmer as "nooning" or resting. At nine in the evening there was a signal for retiring known as curfew. In the earliest days of America when roofs were thatched with grass, this bell asked that all people bank or cover their fires so that they might not flare up during the night. So this bell was called by its French name, *couvre feu* or the "cover-fire bell," and then became the English "curfew bell." The couvre-feu custom of colonial days was also protection against marauding Indians; how strange that our modern word curfew harks back to so primitive a custom.

Just as different cities have different customs, many early villages had their own special bell signals. Those near the sea might tell of rising tides or the arrivals of fishing fleets. Some curfew bells were followed by sharp strokes to indicate the date of the month to aid those making diary entries before retiring for the night. In case of fires, some town bells had a code that told in what area of the countryside the fire was. It was all like a Morse code and it was quite necessary, for there were no other means of communication.

The church bell (never the town bell) tolled death knells, either during the funeral or after the morning town bell had finished. Death knells were "two times three" for a woman and "three times three" for a man. These funeral sounds were all made by hand, with a soft wooden mallet, sometimes known as a "dead striker," and the sound was solemn and muffled. In some places, the deceased's age was tolled (told) by striking that exact number, one strike every minute. Called a "minute bell," this would take an hour and a half for a ninety-one-year-old person.

At Christmas Eve there was a midnight "Devil's Knell" rung for Satan who was said to have "died when Christ was born." Christmas Day ringing in New England began at seven in the morning and ended at four in the afternoon, but the whole day was known as an American Day of Bells.

Although the word *toll* originally meant to "tell," and *knell* indicated sadness, the word knell ceased

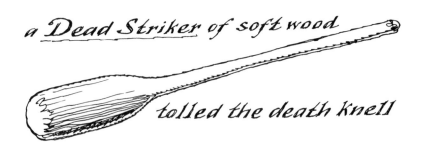

*a Dead Striker of soft wood*

*tolled the death knell*

to be used when funerals were "tolled." Here is an early rhyme which tells something of bell language. Copied from a sampler, it helped children to learn the messages that bells had to tell:

When we lament a departed soul, WE TOLL.
When joy and mirth are on the wing, WE SING.
To call the fold to church in time, WE CHIME.
When threatened harm, WE ALARM.

An alarm was given by a continuous ringing or a steady tattoo (with iron rods) or by grasping the clapper of a handbell and striking it continuously in a quick manner. Anyone hearing such an alarm would consider it a call for immediate help.

With all these bell messages, one might imagine the various codes difficult to learn, and the days all but shattered by the sounds. Yet it was taken for granted, for without bells it would be like our present day without telephones or radio. People enjoyed their town and church bells and they often spoke proudly about "how far their bells could be heard" or about "their rare or fine tone." Some could even foretell the weather by the sound of a distant bell, for when the air pressure lowers as it does before a rain, a bell

*Striking a bell directly and continuously with its own clapper was an old "S.O.S." signal*

does change its tone, sounding as if it were in a long hollow corridor. Under ideal circumstances, the average limit of bell sound is nine miles, but there is one record during a fire alarm, where a bell (in Kennebunk, Maine) was heard plainly eleven miles away (in Alfred, Maine). Generally speaking, a big bell's sound carries better than a rifle shot.

The old-time pranksters had many opportunities with their town and church bells. A favorite April Fool trick was to wrap cloth around the church bell's clapper so that little or no sound came from its striking. Another was to tie a string to the clapper and hiding at a safe distance, to start pulling away at midnight and rouse the whole village.

The Sabbath Day used to be strictly observed, but it was not held during the day of Sunday as it is today; it began at sundown on Saturday and ended at sunset on Sunday. Both the starting and ending times of the Sabbath were rung by the church bell. Knowing how strict and religious the old-timers were, it seems strange that some of the biggest parties were held on Sunday. But, of course, that was after the end of the Sabbath at sundown.

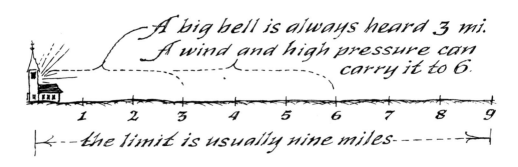

A big bell is always heard 3 mi.
A wind and high pressure can carry it to 6.

1    2    3    4    5    6    7    8    9

←--the limit is usually nine miles------→

# Bells on the Move

People might wonder just why farmers put bells on their animals. We know about cows, of course, and how a belled animal can be located even in a deep forest; yet with a little research we find that cats and dogs and ducks and geese and goats and sheep and even turkeys once had bells of their own design. Some farmers had their cow bells tuned to a certain note so that a lost animal could be identified even at a distance. The lead cow had a huge bell (see drawing) that had a special tone. Geese and turkeys had bells for their own protection as well as identification, for only a century ago the average farm was always troubled with attacks from bears, foxes, wolves, and bobcats.

Most people believe that horse bells were just ornamental and for enjoyment. But bells were a necessary

Sheet metal bells for cows

"a Lead-cow bell"

Wood Cowbells c. 1700

"Navajo" Cow bell with "Cross tongue"

part of winter traffic. Sleighs were fast and silent, while people were usually deafened by earmuffs and mufflers. As there were no sidewalks, people walked in the road, sometimes right in the midst of sleigh traffic, which added to the danger. In a few places in New England, there was even a fine for sleighs that were not properly equipped with bells.

For every wagon he owned, the average farmer of early America had from two to four sleds, for the best roads were those of snow during the winter. During spring and summer, the old dirt roads became

*Horse*

*Team Bells*

snap

*Dog Bells*

c. 1850

*Sheep Bells*

1876
WIGWAM

an impassable sea of mud whenever it rained. Wheels just wouldn't turn under a heavy load on the average cross-country road. So all heavy cargo such as logs

*Earmuffs and mufflers made loud sleighbells necessary.*

or stone was saved till winter and moved easily on runners.

Whereas snow is a present-day nuisance on the streets and highways, at one time in America snow was cherished and saved. It was shoveled from the sides of the road and put into the middle; then it was rolled flat with snow rollers until it was a sheet

*Even the insides of Covered Bridges needed Snow in the old days!*

of ice-like surface which lasted into the spring of the year. Although most people still think the covered bridges were built to keep out the snow, bridge owners were obliged to shovel snow into their bridges so that the sleds could pass through.

Wagon bells jingled and clanged just from the roughness of the road; they were hung either solidly or were on springs. But sleds moved so evenly on the packed snow that bells had to be put on the harness or trappings of the horses, otherwise they would not jingle. Crotal-type bells could be bought by the pound and sewed to leather straps, and the place where they were made was "Jingletown, U.S.A.," East Hampton, Connecticut. This town was (and still is) the bell capital of America. Yankee peddlers went there to pick up crotals to sell along their routes, buying by the pound and selling them singly. Jingletown's catalogs had as many as five hundred kinds and sizes of bells, but the illustration shows four samples from an old Bevin Brothers list.

Sleigh bells (a misnomer because they were usually used on the horses' harness and not the sleigh) have long been the favorite of the American Indian. Even now you will find that a strap of crotals on each ankle is standard costume for any Indian dancer. When there was an Indian attack on a wagon train, sometimes the greatest prizes were the bells that the teams wore.

Actually the bell was the American Indian's natural musical instrument, for from ancient times they made bell-like rattles from gourds and turtle shells and hollow sticks. The "Indian drum" was really introduced by the white soldiers, and there is no record of the very ancient Indian ever having used drums of any kind.

Indians were supposed to be very superstitious about the sound of bells, and women left at home

*The CROTAL was America's sleigh and wagon bell bought by the pound, . . to sew on straps, .. "as many as 500 different kinds".*

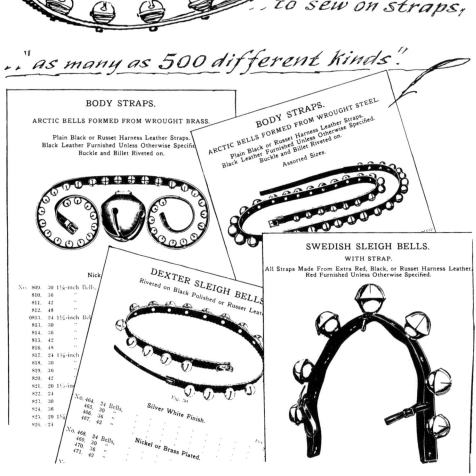

## BODY STRAPS.

### ARCTIC BELLS FORMED FROM WROUGHT BRASS.

Plain Black or Russet Harness Leather Straps.
Black Leather Furnished Unless Otherwise Specified.
Buckle and Billet Riveted on.

## BODY STRAPS.

### ARCTIC BELLS FORMED FROM WROUGHT STEEL.

Plain Black or Russet Harness Leather Straps.
Black Leather Furnished Unless Otherwise Specified.
Buckle and Billet Riveted on.

Assorted Sizes.

## SWEDISH SLEIGH BELLS.

### WITH STRAP.

All Straps Made From Extra Red, Black, or Russet Harness Leather.
Red Furnished Unless Otherwise Specified.

Nick

| | | |
|---|---|---|
| No. 809. | 30 | 1⅝-inch Bells. |
| 810. | 36 | " |
| 811. | 42 | " |
| 812. | 48 | " |
| 0813. | 24 | 1¼-inch Bells |
| 813. | 30 | " |
| 814. | 36 | " |
| 815. | 42 | " |
| 816. | 48 | " |
| 817. | 24 | 1⅜-inch |
| 818. | 30 | " |
| 819. | 36 | " |
| 820. | 42 | " |
| 821. | 20 | 1½-in |
| 822. | 24 | |
| 823. | 30 | |
| 824. | 36 | |
| 825. | 20 | 1⅝ |
| 826. | 24 | |

## DEXTER SLEIGH BELLS

Riveted on Black Polished or Russet Leat

Fig. 30

Silver White Finish.

| | | |
|---|---|---|
| No. 464. | 24 | Bells, |
| 465. | 30 | " |
| 466. | 36 | " |
| 467. | 42 | " |

| | | |
|---|---|---|
| No. 468. | 24 | Bells, |
| 469. | 30 | " |
| 470. | 36 | " |
| 471. | 42 | " |

Nickel or Brass Plated.

during colonial days, often kept a handbell close by, should there be worry about marauding Indians. Ringing the bell gave "an alarm to neighbors and it frightened the savages, at the same time."

The Indians' habit of putting their ear to the ground to hear approaching horses probably gave rise to their superstitions about the bell, for a big town bell can be heard plainly through the ground when often it cannot be heard because of hills or wind interference. There is one legend in New Hampshire about a village that was covered by a winter's avalanche of snow and rocks which completely buried a small church building. "If you put your ear to the ground," so the story goes, "you can still hear the ghostly church bell ring at midnight." Actually what you would hear is the bell from a nearby town, since the sound may carry remarkably well through the ground.

The large handbell used to call children to school is probably the best-known bell in America, and there are people who collect them as Americana. Actually the first American schoolteachers used tin horns for calling children, and so did the housewives when they called the men in from the fields. It might be presumed that there were once so many bells sounding from so many animals and churches and town halls, that a horn was a more commanding and different signal. Horns and even drums were used for calling people to church during the early 1600's. But by the 1700's the bell had become the national instrument for calling people together.

The largest school bell type was used by the town crier. The town crier of the 1600's and early 1700's rang his bell along with his cry of "All's well" in such a manner to comfort rather than alarm people. For alarm or call for help he kept a "rattler," which was a wooden device that made a very loud noise when twirled around. The author has a rattler from Plymouth, Massachusetts which can be easily heard for two miles. The rattler in later years became the alarm for firemen and policemen and night watchmen.

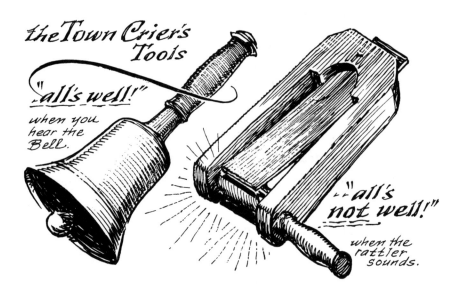

the Town Crier's Tools

"all's well!" when you hear the Bell.

"...all's not well!" when the rattler sounds.

The town crier who roamed the streets calling out the hours was not a typically American figure, but there was a town crier in America who called people together in the town square whenever news arrived. Newspapers seldom printed news in the early days; instead they printed *comments* upon news. The reason for this was, that by the time the news was hand set and printed on the old slow presses, it was no longer news. News, of course, had to arrive by a messenger on horseback. It was immediately put up on a town square bulletin board, and a copy was rushed to the printers. The town crier immediately rang his big bell, and people rushed to the bulletin board to read the news while the newspaper was being printed.

The uses of the bell in America were almost numberless, from devices to scare away birds to buoys at sea and wild animal alarms. Just after the Civil War era, when mass production was introduced and factories began to flourish, inventors found even more uses for bells by putting them into all kinds of mechanical devices. Even now, although we might think the bell an outmoded thing, it wakens you in the morning in your alarm clock, it calls you to the telephone, it ends every line on your typewriter, calls you to the door, and does so many things that we are so used to that we seldom notice them.

*Scare-crow bells*

*pine propellers*

*.. no help unless the wind was blowing*

The bell is still the standard burglar alarm, but people of colonial times used to use a simple handbell at night, balancing it on the mantel or on a chair and tying a string from it to the doorknob. The Yankee peddler sold a little stand for holding a handbell against the door, so it would tip when the door opened; this was called a bell tilt. Farmers often kept a bell in their kitchen garden with a string to the bedroom; a frequent pull on the string whenever the thought came to mind would keep the raccoons or other destructive animals away.

The spring bell was first used on the early fire-fighting wagons. The rough roadways would jounce the wagon and thereby ring the bell. The same idea

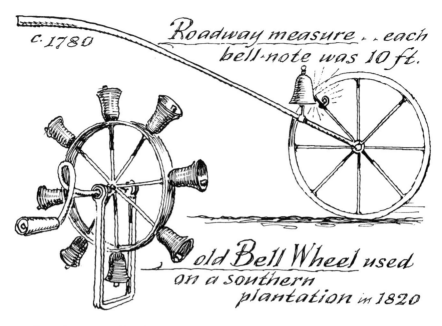

c.1780

Roadway measure...each bell-note was 10 ft.

old Bell Wheel used on a southern plantation in 1820

made the storekeeper's bell jingle whenever a customer opened the door and entered. The call bell was for calling the storekeeper when a customer found the store unattended, but it soon became so handy for calling servants to the table, at hotel desks, etc., that one Bevin Brothers catalog of the 1800's listed 108 different types and sizes of call bells.

And so from such tiny bells as call bells and bicycle bells and tea bells to the giants that made the roofs of surrounding buildings shudder when they spoke, bells have had a peculiar place in the lore and history of America. True, all of our earliest bells came from wrecked ships or across the sea, but from the 1800's on, the American bell makers made themselves

known. The first church bell made by Paul Revere
was done in 1792 and although such early attempts
usually produced bells with poor notes, by the middle
of the 1800's America was manufacturing superior
bells.

Bell makers in America were different from those of
the Old World, for they did their work in a scientific
and businesslike manner, whereas many of the European bell makers chose to attach great mystery to their
work. Perhaps it was to impress the clergy and who-
ever bought their bells, or perhaps because they
really had rare trade secrets and deserved the prom-
inence their strange habits brought to them.

Some bell casters, such as the famous Bilbie family
who made some of the greatest old bells in England,
wore their hair halfway down their backs and practiced strange rites or consulted astrology when making
or tuning their bells. They put in their bell metal

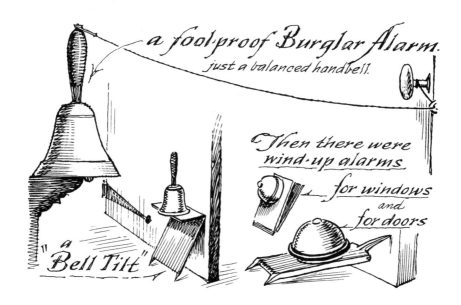

a fool-proof Burglar Alarm.
just a balanced handbell.

Then there were
wind-up alarms
for windows
and
for doors

"a Bell Tilt"

such things as dung, hair, gold coins, and "things that can't be spoken of."

When their bells were ordered to match or be in tune with another group of bells, they were known to ask that the existing bells be rung only before dawn, on a certain day when the atmosphere was "just right." Then submerged naked in a nearby pool, with only his head above water, an expert would command the bell to be rung and listen only after the last ripple had smoothed down from the pool's surface. Bells were always hung and first tried out "when the moon was full."

But none of this mumbo-jumbo nonsense was used by the Americans who made bells. They had printed

*...listening to the bells.*

*...no such mumbo-jumbo from American bell makers!*

catalogs and newspaper advertising just as any other businessmen. By the Civil War era, there came to be a standardized American bell design which many companies manufactured and which came in sizes from "farm size" to "town hall size," schoolhouse and church size. This bell's shoulder was smaller and the lip more flaring than the old European style; many were made simply with mixtures of native irons instead of special bell metal. The drawing shows such a bell along with sizes and prices in the year 1840. Small bells were sold by size, big bells by weight.

With the Civil War many good American customs changed, and among them, the custom of ringing bells on Independence Day. The sounds of guns and

Small shoulder

Flared lip

*American Amalgam Bell 1840* c.

### Farm Bells
15 inch diameter . . . 5.00.
23 inch . . . . . . . . . 12.00

### Church Bells
450 lbs . . . . . . . . . 50.00
850 lbs . . . . . . . . . 100.00

bombs are much louder than that of bells, and America had become used to such noise. When the Civil War ended, firecrackers and aerial bombs had taken over almost completely and only a very few of the "old-fashioned people" were left to ring their bells on the Fourth of July. Some churches carried on the Independence Day custom, although often even the people of the town where they rang were not aware of why the bells were ringing!

# Bombs bursting in air

Fireworks have ruled the "Glorious Fourth" for over a century. They began as just bonfires and gunfire, but the Chinese trade brought firecrackers to America in the 1800's. After Civil War days the country was accustomed to the noise of cannonfire and bombs, and the sound of bells on the Fourth of July became an almost completely forgotten custom.

Japan had entered the fireworks scene by then, and "daytime sky displays" became the great Japanese specialty. The idea was to create all sorts of fantastic shapes in the sky, with smoke. A black burst of smoke might make the body of a big spider, while eight blue streaks of smoke radiating outward would indicate legs. Eagles, cuttlefish, snakes, beehives with bees, flags, and all sorts of wonderful shapes could be made with different kinds of explosions and colored smoke.

... the sky was filled with *Spiders* and *Snakes*

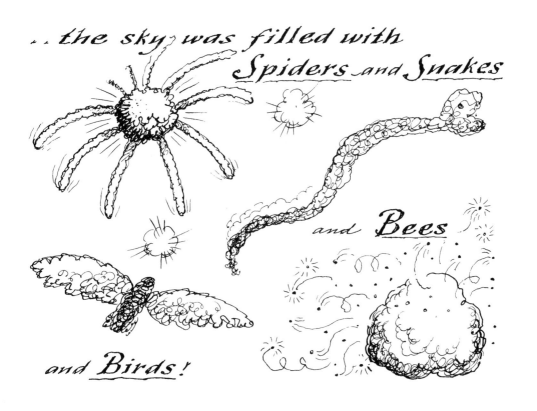

and *Bees*

and *Birds!*

and *Flags*   and *Fish*

and *Comets*   and *Cats*

The Japanese, who were already expert at kite-making with tissue paper, found that bird shapes and fish shapes and flags and parachutes could be burst into the air by rocket, to float down very slowly, to the delight of everyone.

The basis for fireworks was different mixtures of *sulphur, charcoal,* and *potassium nitrate,* but colors could be introduced by adding nitrate of strontia for red, nitrate of soda for yellow, nitrate of baryta for green, and sulphate of copper for blue. Steel, iron, copper, and zinc filings produced sparks of various colors. Even before skyrockets became the popular Independence Day skypiece, "pyrotechnic signal balloons" were set aloft during the daytime, carrying slow-fused smoke bombs and colored lights.

These contraptions were too big and complicated and costly, but the idea of smaller hot-air paper balloons stuck, and they soon became the first pieces that ascended into the night sky on the Fourth. Just a big red, white, and blue tissue paper bulb shape, with wire to hold the mouth open, and a wad of alcohol-soaked material furnishing the heat, these ballons could reach a height of two thousand feet and stay aloft for over an hour. They seemed to fill in that tense hour or two when everyone was waiting for the sky to get dark enough to set off the nighttime rockets. The sight of balloon lights, like little

first piece into the night sky... the *Balloon*

wad of cotton soaked with alcohol.

stars, made the Independence Day sunset a most memorable one.

Balloon time on the Fourth, during the late 1800's and early 1900's, was also the signal for lighting lanterns. People had to see their way around the lawns and verandas. Even if there had been electric lights, they would have shattered the romantic, festive illusion that candles and oil lights brought to any outdoor fete.

What candlelight is to a banquet, colored lamps,

parade torches, and Japanese lanterns were to the old-time Fourth of July night. Copying a Mexican custom, paper bags were sometimes weighted with sand and used as "luminarias" to light walks and driveways or even to outline houses and boathouses. Indeed, in the old days, the night had a special magic and beauty of its own. Singing around a bonfire, picnicking and making the night alive with colored lights seem to be lost arts.

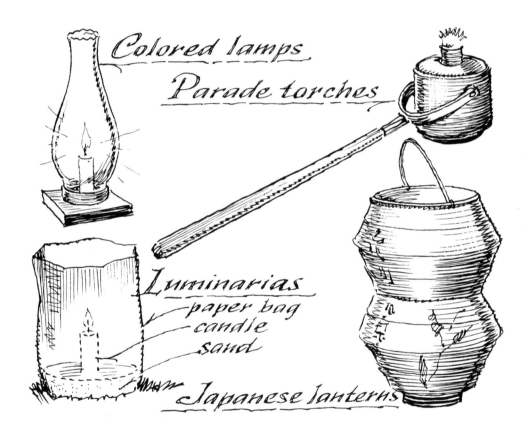

Colored lamps

Parade torches

Luminarias
—paper bag
—candle
sand

Japanese lanterns

Fireworks, in the old days, were expensive even at a penny a salute, and this was brought home by the quickness of their performance. Even at the height of a rocket's course there was always the twinge of having been a spendthrift, and when the rocket finally burst with a thunderous bang, there was the thought, "Well, there goes another dollar!"

For the smaller children there were sulphur "snakes" which when lit would grow into amazingly

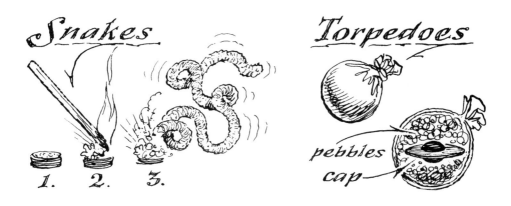

long snake-like forms. There were torpedoes that blew up when you threw them down on the sidewalk. During the early 1900's these simple cap-in-pebble devices grew into pretty dangerous "cherry bombs" that were loud enough to wake up a whole neighborhood. It was all dangerous but it was fun.

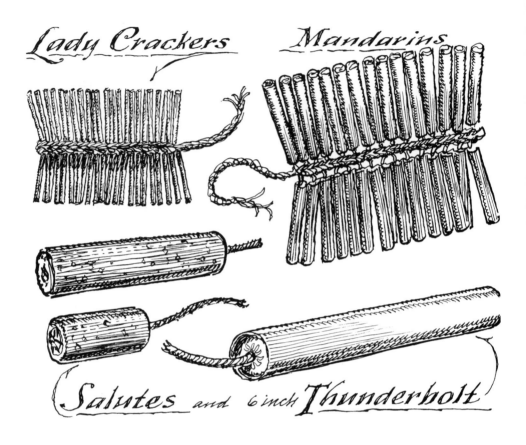

*Lady Crackers*   *Mandarins*

*Salutes and 6 inch Thunderbolt*

There were lady crackers that went off like machine-gun fire, bigger "mandarin"-size firecrackers, salutes in thick cardboard, and big six-inch thunderbolts that went off like cannons. Set off under a flat rock, they could turn the rock over; set off under a tin can, they would send the can some thirty feet up. Thrown into water, they would send a spray in every direction for about twenty feet. What could be more exciting?

*Lifting the can...*

You could order your fireworks in sets from a big catalog that a boy could pore through even months before the big event. The names of the night pieces were always fantastic and exciting to the imagination. There were several sizes of "Vesuvius Cascades," "Devil-among-the-tailors," "Whistling Dragons," "Niagara Fountains," "Roman Candles," "Bengal Lights," "Golden Rain," and "Exploding Comets." The boxes they came in were of new white wood that smelled of fresh excelsior and sawdust and the firework pieces would emerge in Chinese gold-flecked paper wrappings.

Just as Christmas has its unwrapping of packages, Independence Day used to have its ceremony of opening packages to lay out on the lawn, ready for proper sequence at the night display. All day long there was the smell of punk, the tang of gunpowder in the air, and the smoldering of cardboard. It was almost as much fun laying out the night pieces as it was setting them off. And when the morning of July fifth arrived, there was always the search for duds, interesting remains, or those that just missed getting fired off. It was a day to be remembered.

Perhaps only mother wanted to forget it, for the Fourth of July was a man's day and except for watching the night display, mother's only participation was

...the sounds of Peace....

to take care of the burns and apply the bandages.

We who remember when Fourth of July fireworks were sold everywhere in the United States miss the fun of shooting them off, but we shall be first to admit that they do make the sound of war, and that bells make a sound of peace and freedom. After all, the sounds of peace are not always loud noises; they are more often like those comforting sounds of America when it was young. Even the Liberty Bell, which is so old and cracked that now it cannot be rung or even struck with a hammer for fear that it might shatter and fall apart, is nevertheless heard in its completely quiet way, in every corner of the civilized world today.

# The LIBERTY Bell

*that started out as the "Penn Jubilee Bell"*

There is a bell that millions of people travel to Philadelphia to see. They touch it with reverence, knowing that they are touching something sacred to the national history. Some stare at it and suddenly burst into tears without really knowing why. Once two blind Japanese soldiers in uniform came "to see" the bell and asked the guide to read the inscription thereon; but the guide led their hands over the raised letters and showed them where the crack was. The guide watched them leave, talking in their own language, and he wondered what they really thought of the bell and its legend. But stuffed carefully in the bell's crack, he found two roses that the veterans had been wearing.

There once was a custom that men remove their hats in the presence of the Liberty Bell, and some still do that. For a bell that does not ring, it is evident that it has become more symbol than bell; perhaps the sound it made in 1776 was strong enough to be heard today by all the peoples of the world.

The bell does not ring because the slightest stroke might shatter the ancient metal into pieces; the last time it was heard, it was struck softly with a rubber mallet. A few years ago, a man in a red fez shouted profanity and struck the bell with a heavy glass paperweight. It nicked the bell metal, and the man was taken away to a mental institution. Recently there was a plot to dynamite the bell.

It is strange that this is perhaps the most well-known bell in the world, yet it is also the one with the least-known history. Very many Americans believe it was made for the occasion of the signing of the Declaration of Independence, or at least that it was made a year or so before the War for Independence.

A controversy is whether it rang at all on July 4, 1776, and the reason for questioning is merely that "there are no records of it having rung on that day." Of course, as the object of that bell was to call people to meeting and to announce the end of each meeting, it was not at all necessary to record every time the bell rang. If the Liberty Bell did not call to meeting on that July 4, and ring the end of that meeting, it would have been unusual indeed. We must presume without doubt that the Liberty Bell rang at least some time on that day. And as the whole town was waiting outside to hear news about the Declaration (and there was no reason for its preparation being secret), those who insist the bell was silent are presuming something very strange. Of course, the Liberty Bell and many other American bells rang when the Declaration was read on the eighth of July, 1776, and all the following July 4— the day finally decided upon to be known as Independence Day.

It is a pity that the history of the great bell has been argued about so much that it has joined the category of doubtful Americana (like the Betsy Ross legend), for its true story is exciting and even more American than most people realize. It started twenty-five years before the Declaration of Independence, and it was ordered to commemorate another declaration called The Charter of Privileges, issued in 1701.

Now in those days when the country was so young, there could not be many hundred-year anniversaries or "centennials"; but there were some fifty-year celebrations that were called jubilees. In fact, the word jubilee once meant a fiftieth-year celebration. The word fifty seemed to have a magic significance to it, and in

Pennsylvania one could vote if he owned fifty acres or had fifty pounds in money; land leases were made out for fifty years, and the fifty acres' dowry was an accepted custom. So when the fiftieth anniversary of the William Penn Charter of Privileges neared in 1751, it seemed a good time for a great jubilee.

This fiftieth-year jubilee was to be in many ways like our present Independence Day, celebrated with bells, gunshots, bonfires by day, and illuminations at night. But the people found some difficulty in choosing a symbol for their jubilee. "Why not make a bell, and inscribe upon it the quotation from Leviticus? Besides, the State House needs a bell."

Nearly everyone was familiar with the Leviticus quotation (25:10) that went, "and ye shall hallow the fiftieth year . . . and it shall be a jubilee unto you." And so it was decided to make a commemorative bell with this quotation upon it.

And then a strange course of events took place. First, it was found that there were no craftsmen in America who made such bells, so the new bell would have to be made in England. But there wasn't enough time, for before the order could reach England and the bell be made and shipped back, the jubilee would be over and forgotten. It was decided that the order go through, but the inscription be changed slightly, taking out that part which mentioned the "fiftieth year" and the reference to "a jubilee."

Isaac Norris, who was Speaker of the Assembly, did the editing, and little did he know that the result would some day refer to another declaration twenty-five years hence. It made the bell not only commemorative of a jubilee but the symbol of a new nation. Here then is the Leviticus quotation (the capital letters spell out what remained after the deletion):

"And ye shall hallow the fiftieth year and PROCLAIM LIBERTY THROUGHOUT ALL THE LAND UNTO ALL THE INHABITANTS THEREOF: it shall be a jubilee unto you and shall return every man unto his possession, and ye shall return every man unto his family."

The bell was cast in early 1752 at the Whitechapel Foundry in England and delivered in the summer of that year, and it was set up in the State House yard for testing. But when it was rung for tone, a crack appeared and the moans of despair were almost as loud as the sound of the bell. The Assembly was going to return it to England, but two workmen offered to melt it and cast it again. "After all," they said, "such a symbol of religious freedom should be made right here in Pennsylvania and not in England. We think we can do a good job."

Actually, they failed to do a good job, for when John Pass and John Stow tested out their new bell, it cracked again. But they tried again, adding 1½ ounces of copper for each pound of the old bell's

Respected Friend Robt Charles                    Philada Novr 1st. 1751

The Assembly having ordered us ( the Superintendants of our Statehouse ) to procure a Bell from England to be purchased for their use we take the Liberty to apply ourselves to thee to get us a good Bell of about two thousand pounds weight the cost of which we presume may amount to abt One hundred pounds Sterl. or perhaps with the the Charges something more and accordingly we have now inclosed a first Bill of Excha girt John Perrin and Son on Messrs Thomas Howardens & Compa for £100 — Sterling. We would have chosen to remit a larger Bill at this time, but will take care to furnish more as soon as we can be informed how much may be wanted

We hope and rely on thy care and assistances in this affair and that thou wilt procure and forward it by the first good oppo as our Workmen inform us it will be much less trouble to hang the Bell before their Scaffolds are struck from the Building where we intend to place it which will not be done till the end of next Summer or beginning of the Hall . Let the Bell be cast by the best Workmen & examined carefully before it is Shipped with the following words well shaped in large letters round it vizt
BY order of the Assembly of the Province of Pensylvania for the Statehouse in the City of Philada 1752 and Underneath.
Proclaim Liberty thro all the Land to all the Inhabitants thereof Levit XXV.10 —

As we have experienced thy readiness to Serve this province on all occasions We Desire it may be our excuse for this additional trouble from

                                        Thy Assured Frds

Let the package for transportation be examined          { Isaac Norris
with particular care. and the full value   Signed by an { Thomas Leech
Insured thereon                                         { Edward Warner

metal, and this time the bell was sound. It was the first time anything like this had been done in America, and when the bell was hung in State House a great feast began in the yard below. There is a record that shows three hundred limes (for punch), three gallons of rum, a barrel of beer, three pecks of potatoes, forty-four pounds of beef, a fifteen-pound cheese, and a band of musicians.

The famous bell seemed to ring louder than most bells. Indeed, there were complaints from nearby townspeople. In a petition to the Assembly, the bell was named "a lethal object" and that because of its "unusual size and sound, it might prove fatal to those afflicted with sickness." Nevertheless it continued to call statesmen to meeting and then announce the end of each session. Muffled (as in a funeral toll) it announced each British tax outrage; it rang loudly with the news of Lexington and Concord.

On July 4, 1777, the Liberty Bell pealed forth defiance when the British were preparing an attack

*Philadelphia in a load of Hay*

on Philadelphia. On September 14, the Continental Congress realized the danger of invasion and resolved to move all bells from the city, knowing that the British would seek out metal for cannon barrels and ammunition. Where the bells were hidden was kept such a secret that to this day there is doubt about where the Liberty Bell really went. We do know that it left Philadelphia in a caravan of farm wagons, most likely hidden under a load of hay.

Legend has it that the bell was taken to Allentown and hidden beneath the floor of a church. Another story is that the wagon broke under the weight and the bell fell off at Bethlehem, where it was secreted. But there are so many stories about the route taken, that scores of towns in Pennsylvania are known for being the town where the bell was hidden, or through which the bell passed. The truth will never be known. But in the summer of 1778, the bells of Philadelphia were returned, and in 1781 the Liberty Bell, back in its tower, pealed the surrender of Cornwallis at Yorktown.

Some people believe that great bells become humanized with a conscience and that the Liberty Bell always resented the shortening of its Leviticus quotation. Indeed, there have been some strange coincidences connected with the bell's history that might

Ordered in 1751 . . .

cast in
London 1752 . . .
Philadelphia 1753

bear out such an eerie argument. It managed, for example, to toll the death of all signers of the Declaration of Independence, but when the fiftieth-year jubilee of Independence Day arrived, (July 4, 1826), it tolled the death of both John Adams and Thomas Jefferson. Hardly before one death knell had finished, the toll for the other great man began. It was a startling finish to a jubilee.

In 1835 on July eighth, the anniversary of the bell's biggest day, it tolled the death of John Marshall, the last of the Federalist statesmen who shaped the early Republic. At that moment it cracked.

# Postscript

In this day of free verse and abstract art, the painting or writing that tells a complete story is sometimes considered what young people call "square." "Square" and "corny" and "old-fashioned" are words that are often used to belittle things which, when you really think about them, are basic and soul-stirring. The Boy Scouts, the Girl Scouts, the Stars and Stripes, the National Anthem and all the things that keep America alive in the secret corners of our hearts, sometimes bringing a tear of emotion, are frequently considered childish and "square." Of course during war, we display more patriotism; but when times are good, Washington's Birthday is just a sale day at the department stores and Independence Day is a day for fun at the beach and the ball field. Yet at one time such patriotic days had much more meaning. They told a story of America.

*The Sound of Bells* was written with a purpose, and I hope that the reader will have agreed with me that America's birthday (Independence Day) should be more special and significant than most people regard it. Ringing a bell on July Fourth may seem pretty childish, but it is a beginning. And if the revival of the early American custom of ringing bells on Independence Day will have become established, I would consider this one thing the most important occurrence connected with my life.

In 1963 a resolution passed by the U. S. Congress asks that all bells in the nation, church bells, school bells, town bells, ring together for four minutes at 2 P.M. (E.D.T.) on July Fourth, and governors in their yearly Independence Day proclamations, name the day as a day for the ringing of bells.

If this book adds in any way to the establishment of the custom, I shall be most grateful.

Eric Sloane

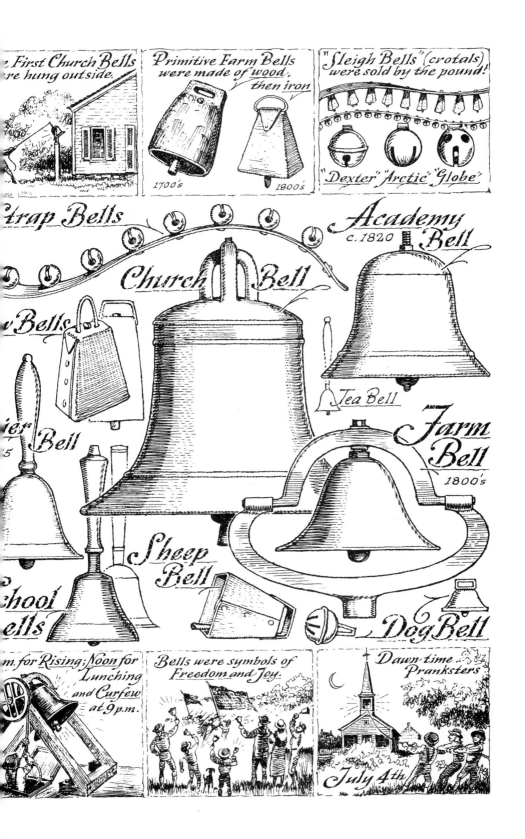

First Church Bells were hung outside.

Primitive Farm Bells were made of wood, then iron

1700's

1800's

"Sleigh Bells" (crotals) were sold by the pound!

"Dexter" "Arctic" "Globe"

Strap Bells

Academy Bell
c. 1820

Church Bell

Cow Bells

Tea Bell

Farm Bell
1800's

Dinner Bell

Sheep Bell

School Bells

Dog Bell

...m. for Rising; Noon for Lunching and Curfew at 9 p.m.

Bells were symbols of Freedom and Joy.

Dawn-time Pranksters

July 4th

## Other books by Eric Sloane available as Dover reprints*

Return to Taos: Eric Sloane's Sketchbook of Roadside
　Americana

Eric Sloane's Book of Storms: Hurricanes, Twisters and
　Squalls

Skies and the Artist

The Little Red Schoolhouse

For Spacious Skies: A Sketchbook of American Weather

Do's and Don't of Yesteryear: A Treasury of Early
　American Folk Wisdom

A Museum of Early American Tools

American Barns and Covered Bridges

American Yesterday

A Reverence for Wood

Look at the Sky and Tell the Weather

Our Vanishing Landscape

Diary of an Early American Boy: 1805

The Seaon's of America Past

The Cracker Barrel

Once Upon a Time: The Way America Was

Eric Sloane's Weather Book

Recollections in Back and White

* Log on to **www.doverpublications.com** for more information.